Saw,
Hammer,
and
Paint

Woodworking
and Finishing
for Beginners

SAW, HAMMER, AND PAINT

by Carolyn Meyer

ILLUSTRATED BY TONI MARTIGNONI

William Morrow and Company
New York 1973

Meyer, Carolyn.
  Saw, hammer, and paint.

  SUMMARY: A guide to woodworking with directions
and diagrams for numerous projects ranging in diffi-
culty from a cheese board to a desk.
    1. Woodwork—Juvenile literature. 2. Wood finishing
—Juvenile literature. [1. Woodwork. 2. Wood finishing]
I. Martignoni, Toni, illus. II. Title.
TT185.M46   684/08   72-9927
ISBN 0-688-20069-9
ISBN 0-688-30069-3 (lib. bdg.)

FOR ALAN, JOHN, AND CHRISTOPHER

Contents

INTRODUCTION   7

I WOODWORKING   9
1 WHAT YOU WILL NEED   10
Wood   10
Supplies   13
Tools   14
2 GETTING STARTED   19
Measuring and Marking   19
Cutting   20
Making a Cheeseboard   24
Sanding   25
3 GLUING THINGS TOGETHER   27
Using Glue   27
Making a Candlestick   28
Making a Tray   32
Cutting a Mitered Corner   34
4 NAILING THINGS TOGETHER   37
Driving Nails   37
Making a House Number
· Sign with Nails   39
Toeing Nails 40
Making an Assemblage with Nails   41
Making a Butt Joint   43
Using a Working Drawing
   and a Bill of Materials   43
Laying out Your Work   45
Making a Five-sided Cube   46
Countersinking Nails   54

Making a Ten-inch Cube   56
Upholstering a Seat   58
Making a Sixteen-inch Cube   59
Putting a Lid on the Cube   61
Using Hinges   62
Making a Sewing Box   65
Putting Another Kind of Lid on a Box   69
Making a Card File   70
Making a Miniature House   72
5 SCREWING THINGS TOGETHER   78
Drilling Screw Holes   78
Making a Bench   80
Making a Bookcase   82
Understanding More
    about Working Drawings   85
Making a Cabinet with a Door   88
Hanging the Door   90
Making a Drawer   91
Fitting the Drawer in
    the Cabinet or Bookcase   94
Making a Desk   95

II WOOD FINISHING   99
1 CHOOSING A BASIC FINISH   100
Using an Oil Finish   104
Coloring Wood with Stain   106
Varnishing   109
Painting   111
Painting with Two Colors   116
2 ADDING A DECORATIVE FINISH   118
Stenciling   118
Glazing   121
Decoupage   123

Introduction

Wood is one of the most practical as well as beautiful of all the materials that people have ever used for constructing things. It has been used for building houses and barns, bridges and ships. It has been used for making useful objects like clothespins and rulers, amusing things like toys and dolls, furniture that is both elegant and functional, and musical instruments that both look and sound beautiful.

The beauty of wood has always made it especially appealing to artists. In the Middle Ages, artists carved and painted statues and altar pieces of wood for the great churches of Europe. In the early days of America, carved wooden Indians advertised the presence of cigar stores. Louise Nevelson is an important American artist who constructs very large sculptures from wooden objects, such as chair legs and knobs, and then paints the sculptures all one color. Marisol, another artist whose work is exhibited in many museums, puts together great blocks of wood to form sculptures. Then she paints them with the features of people and animals.

Sophisticated machinery now mass-produces wooden objects at high speed. Wood is so popular that conservationists fear we may one day run out of timber unless more steps are taken to replace the trees that are cut down. Recently, plastic and metal have begun to replace wood for many things—houses and barns, bridges and ships, clothespins and toys, and even in art. Besides being tough and long-lasting, plastic and metal have a beauty of their own, though they are harder to work with than wood and require more elaborate tools. But there is nothing really that quite matches the beauty of wood carefully handled and finely finished.

The projects in this book were designed so that both boys and girls would enjoy making them. With simple hand tools, inexpensive wood, and a little practice, you can turn out useful, handsome objects that you'll be proud of.

Part I
WOODWORKING

CHAPTER ONE

What You Will Need

WOOD

Everybody knows that wood comes from trees. Not everyone knows that wood from different kinds of trees not only looks different and has different uses but is handled differently too.

Generally, there are two types of wood. **Hardwood**—the wood is hard and heavy as well—comes from deciduous trees, which shed their broad leaves every year. Walnut, oak, and maple are hardwoods.

Softwood is easier to cut and drive nails and screws into. Conifers—trees that bear cones and needles instead of leaves—yield the softwoods, such as pine, fir, redwood, and cedar.

But some hardwoods are actually rather soft and easy to work with, while some softwoods seem quite hard. For a simple test, press the edge of your thumbnail into the wood. If it leaves a mark, it is probably a softwood.

You can learn to identify wood by its grain, the distinctive pattern of stripes and markings that runs through it. Color is another identifying mark. Redwood, for example, is reddish brown. Black walnut is dark purplish brown. Fir is light and yellowish. Pine is a little darker.

When you decide to make something of wood, start gathering supplies. Of course, you can simply go to a lumberyard and buy what you need, and at times that may be the only way to get the wood you want.

But there are other sources. If your father or mother or some other person in the family enjoys working with wood, you may find scraps left from their projects. Perhaps someone in your neighborhood is building a new house or fixing up an old one and has leftover wood to give you. If you live in a city apartment, maybe the superintendent has some scraps.

Lumberyards often have leftover pieces they may give you or sell for less than the regular price. Carpenters and cabinetmakers in your town might be willing to let you have odds and ends of wood.

You'll find that wood, which is often called *stock,* comes in many different forms. These are some of them:

Lumber: Most wood is usually cut into boards of various widths, thicknesses, and lengths. In buying wood, you'll notice something odd about the measurements. When you ask for a board 1″ thick and 6″ wide, the one you get will be a little thinner and narrower.

The original rough board *was* 1″ x 6″,

but it has been planed down, or smoothed, so that the *actual* measurements are always a little less than the *nominal,* or original, measurements. Be sure to tell the salesman the actual size you need for a project so that he can sell you the correct nominal size. Lengths usually come in multiples of two feet.

Plywood: Very thin sheets of wood, called *veneers,* that are glued together in layers, or plies, under pressure, with the grains alternating. For instance, in 3-ply plywood, the outside, or face, veneer has the grain running lengthwise. The grain of the middle, or core, runs crosswise.

The resulting "sandwich" of wood plies is very strong. Plywood comes in large rectangles, usually 4′ wide by 6′ or 8′ long, and from ⅛″ to 1″ thick (in plywood, all the thicknesses are actual).

The face veneers of plywood are of better quality than the inside, or core, layers. Sometimes the top veneer is of very fine wood, like teak, which comes from southeast Asia. A solid piece of teak is extremely expensive, but a teak veneer on plywood is just as handsome and costs much less.

Paneling: Wood precut by special machinery into panels suitable for a particular use. For instance, large, rather thin sheets of wood are used to cover walls, especially in remodeling rooms. The sheets have grooves running from top to bottom to give the appearance of individual pieces of wood.

Molding: Wood cut in long, narrow strips that are glued or nailed on flat surfaces to cover joints where pieces of wood come together. Fancy strips are used on doors or drawers for decoration or finishing.

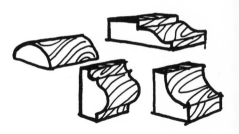

Hardboard: A material, scarcely recognizable as wood, made by pressing wood fibers into large sheets 1/4" or 1/2" thick. It is sold under trade names like Masonite and has a very smooth surface especially good for painting.

SUPPLIES

In addition to wood of different kinds, you'll need a few simple supplies.

Glue: Any white household glue, like Elmer's Glue-All or Solomon's Sobo Glue, is suitable.

Sandpaper: Heavy paper, about 9" x 11", coated on one side with a gritty substance (not really sand, but particles of aluminum oxide, flint, or garnet) is used to smooth wood for finishing. It ranges from very rough to very fine. You'll need two grades: one for rough sanding and another for fine.

Nails: There are different sizes and kinds for different uses. Common nails with broad, flat heads are used where they don't show. Finishing nails and brads have small

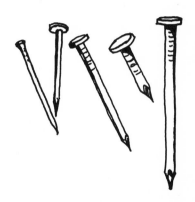

heads and are used on surfaces that are visible.

Screws: These come with round heads and flat heads. Roundheads, whose tops stick up from the surface, are generally used for decoration. Flatheads stay even with the surface and are used when screws are not to show. You'll be using slotted flatheads for the projects in this book. (Another kind, called a Phillips screw, has a cross slot in the head and requires a special screwdriver.) Screw sizes are given by length and by a number that indicates the diameter, or thickness, of the screw. You will use #6 or #8 wood screws for most of your work. As a general rule, the screw should be long enough to go almost the same distance through both pieces to be joined.

Wood putty: A soft, claylike material is used to fill in nail holes or holes and deep scratches in the wood. After it hardens, it can be sanded and finished like wood.

Hardware: As you work on more elaborate projects, you'll need various kinds of hardware, such as hinges, handles, and knobs.

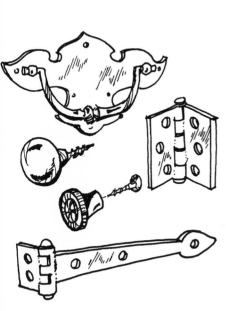

TOOLS

All the projects described in this book can be made with simple hand tools. If you need to borrow any, take especially good care of them. Keep them clean, and remember to return them promptly or put them back where they belong. Tools left lying around can become damaged, and they can be dangerous too. Rust will ruin tools in a very short time, especially when they are left outdoors. Before you put them away or return them, wipe them with an oily cloth. Any kind of oil will do—motor oil or even vegetable oil from the kitchen.

If you are buying your own tools, invest in good quality, which pays in the long run. A cheap saw, for example, dulls very quickly, and trying to cut with a dull saw can be a frustrating experience.

Craftsmen know there's a proper tool for every job and that using the right tool makes their work easier and better. However, you can often substitute when you have to.

Rule: You'll be using one constantly to measure, to check measurements, and to draw lines. Carpenters and woodworkers generally use a metal rule, but you can also use a wooden yardstick. A standard 12″ wooden ruler is good for short measurements.

Pencil: A carpenter's pencil with a thick point and soft lead is best for marking cutting lines and measurements and for labeling the back of each piece you cut. An ordinary pencil can be used instead.

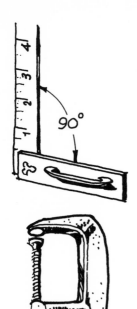

Whichever you use, keep the point sharp.

Square: This L-shaped piece of metal is used to check that corners and the surfaces they connect are absolutely square. It comes in several sizes, and the small version, called a *try square,* is adequate for your purposes. You can also use the corner of anything you are sure is perfectly square, such as a right-angled plastic or metal triangle.

Clamp or vise: Either of these will hold the wood firmly while you are working on it. The carpenter's bench you may be working at probably has a vise permanently attached. Otherwise use 2 C-clamps (the 4″ size will do).

Hand saw: A *rip saw,* with teeth set at an angle, is used for cutting a piece of wood in the direction of the grain. A *crosscut saw,* with straight teeth, or points, is used for cutting across the grain. It can also be used for ripping, although it cuts slowly. A crosscut saw with 8 or 10 points per inch is the right size for the work you'll be doing.

RIP SAW

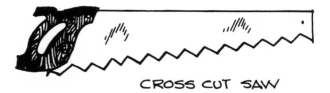

CROSS CUT SAW

Hammer: Hammers come in a variety of weights and styles. Get a *claw hammer,* with the forked end of the hammerhead designed for pulling out nails. The 10-ounce size is probably the correct weight for you. A heavier one is harder to handle.

Hand drill: This tool, which looks and operates like an eggbeater, is used to drill a hole through a piece of wood in which you are using screws. It keeps the wood from splitting and also makes the work easier. Bits—the actual cutting parts—for the drill come in a variety of sizes so that you can drill the size hole you want. Small bits, 1/8″ or less, will be fine for your work.

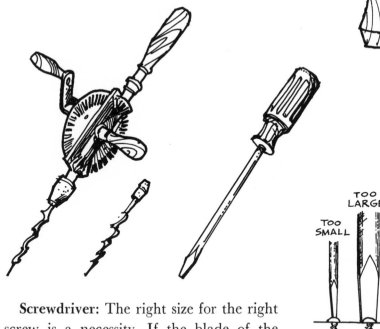

TOO
LARGE

TOO
SMALL

JUST
RIGHT

Screwdriver: The right size for the right screw is a necessity. If the blade of the screwdriver is too thick, it won't fit into the slot in the screw head. If it is wider than the slot, it will scratch the wood as it gets closer to the surface. If the blade is too small, it will twist in the slot and scratch the metal screw. The wrong size is also likely to slip, and that is dangerous. Longer screwdrivers have more driving power.

Awl, or punch: This sharp instrument, which looks like an ice pick, is used to pierce a small hole in which to start driving a nail or drilling a hole. If you don't have one, use a thin nail.

Nail set: Use this tapered tool to drive nails below the surface of the wood so the heads can be hidden with wood putty. You can also use a large nail.

Putty knife: A knife with a broad flexible blade is used to work putty into nail holes and to smooth the surfaces. You can also use a screwdriver or an old dinner knife, or press the putty in with your thumb.

CHAPTER TWO

Getting Started

MEASURING AND MARKING

Before you begin measuring, check to make sure there are no knots, cracks, or other flaws in the wood you are using.

If you are cutting a piece from a board, use a square to make sure the end of the board has perfectly square corners.

Fit the corner of the board snugly inside the angle of the square, with the long leg of the square firmly along the edge of the board and the short leg across the end. If it fits well, the corners are square.

But if you can see any light between the square and the end of the board, you must cut off the uneven end. Lay the square on the board with its outside edge exactly even with the edge of the board. Hold it firmly in place and use the top edge of the square as a guide for drawing a cutting line.

For better accuracy, measure and cut one line at a time before you measure the next one.

If the piece you need is narrower than the board, measure from the edge of the board to the width you want. Make 2 pencil marks at widely spaced intervals and connect them with a line drawn along the edge of a rule or a yardstick.

Carpenters have an old saying: "Measure twice, cut once." And, of course, make sure you're reading the measurement correctly, so you don't cut the wrong size and perhaps turn a good piece of wood into scrap.

In woodworking, measurements are always shown as " for inches and ' for feet. For instance, ¼" x 6" x 24" means ¼ inch thick by 6 inches wide by 24 inches long; 4' x 6' means 4 feet wide by 6 feet long. In lumber measurements, feet and inches are not mixed; you would not say ¼" x 6" x 2'.

CUTTING

To make a straight and even cut, and to do it the safe way, the wood must be held firmly while you saw.

If the board from which you want to cut a piece is rather short—say, less than 4'— fasten it flat to your worktable with a C-clamp or put it in a vise if you have one.

Position it so that the board sticks out far enough past the edge of the table so the clamp and the table edge won't be in the way of the saw as you cut.

Before you tighten the clamp, slip 2 thin pieces of wood or cardboard between the jaws of the clamp and the board to keep the jaws from marking the wood.

Stand with the table to your left (to your right, if you are left-handed) and the projecting piece of wood in front of you.

The clamped board should be at about hip level when you are sawing. If it is higher, stand on a sturdy box or a low stool.

To begin the cut, rest the teeth of the saw against the edge of the board at a 45-degree angle. That means the saw should not be held either straight up and down or level with the wood but about halfway between those two positions. The saw should be to the right of the pencil cutting line,

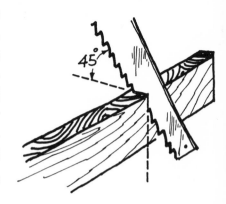

barely touching it. For a guide in starting the cut, place a small block of wood at the edge of the board against the blade of the saw. With your left hand on the guide block, pull the saw back toward you—an upstroke. Then push it away—a downstroke. Try to keep it at the 45-degree angle, and make long, even strokes. You don't have to press on the saw—its weight helps to cut on the downstroke.

Be careful not to twist the saw or allow it to lean to either side or it will not cut smoothly.

After you have the cut well started, you can discard the guide block. Then with your left hand reach across and hold the piece you're sawing off. Be sure to stay to the left of the saw, so that when it cuts through the last bit of wood it doesn't slip and cut *you*.

Learning to keep the saw on the cutting line comes with practice. If you watch carefully, you will see immediately when the saw is starting to stray off course. Maybe you will find that you are cutting into the pencil line or that a hairline of wood is beginning to show between the pencil line and the saw.

If you catch a straying cut at that point, you can correct it just by pressing the saw in the direction you want it to go. You'll learn to "feel" how much pressure you should apply.

But if the mistake has become a serious one, go back to the point where it first began and try to correct it. If you have cut *into* the piece you need, you may have spoiled it for that use. (Perhaps you can use it later by cutting a smaller piece from it.)

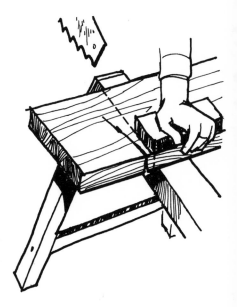

But if you have cut *away* from the piece you need, you can go back a little and start a new cut closer to the line. Use your guide block until the new cut has been well started.

When you are cutting from a very long board or a piece of plywood or paneling, lay the wood across 2 sawhorses, chairs, or sturdy stools.

In this setup the longest part of the board and one horse are on your left, your left knee (if you are right-handed) is holding down the board over the second horse, and the piece you are cutting off is on your right.

Don't try to make the cut in the wood between the 2 sawhorses. The wood is not supported, and it can break as you saw through it. That's bad for the wood and dangerous for you.

If the piece you are cutting off is large, place a support under it while you are sawing. If it is small, you can reach across and support it with your left hand.

Use your full weight when you kneel on the board to keep it from shifting. Use a guide block until the cut is started. Saw all

the way across the board, even if you need
only a small piece.

MAKING A CHEESE BOARD

You can make a board for cutting and
serving cheese simply by cutting a piece of
wood to the size you want and then finishing it.

Use a piece of wood about ¾″ or 1″

thick, with a nice grain and free of knot-holes or cracks. You can make whatever size cheese board you want, but 8″ x 10″ is about as small as it should be. That means you will need a piece of wood at least 8″ wide. A pine board would be perfect.

Use a try square to square the end of the board.

Measure the correct length and mark it. Draw a cutting line, using a rule as a guide.

Clamp the wood to your worktable and saw it along the cutting line. Remember to saw just to the right of the cutting line rather than directly on it.

Measure the correct width and mark it. Draw a cutting line. Use a try square to be sure the line you have drawn makes a perfect square with the edge.

Clamp the wood and saw it.

Now you are ready for finishing, but first you must smooth the wood by sanding.

SANDING

In any project, no matter what kind of finish you put on the wood, it must be clean and smooth. The best way to smooth a wood surface is with sandpaper.

Begin with rough sandpaper. Fold a sheet in half, rough side out, and tear it on the fold. (Don't cut it—it will ruin the scissors.) Use a table edge or the edge of a rule to

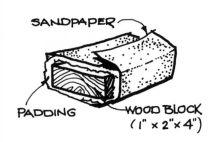

SANDPAPER

PADDING WOOD BLOCK
(1" x 2" x 4")

make a straight tear. Then tear the 2 halves in half again so that you end up with 4 pieces, each about 4½" x 5½".

Sandpaper is easier to handle if you use a sanding block. Find (or cut) a piece of wood about 2" x 4" and about 1" thick. Wrap the piece of sandpaper around the block. A padding of felt or foam between the block and the sandpaper provides a resilient backing and makes sanding easier.

Lay the piece of wood flat on the worktable and rub the sanding block evenly back and forth on the wood in the direction of the grain. Always sand with the grain. If you sand across the grain, you'll scratch the wood.

Next sand the edges, then the ends. If possible, clamp the wood so that you can use both hands to sand with even strokes.

After a thorough rough sanding, switch to a fine grade of sandpaper and sand again. Hold the piece of wood to the light and feel it with your fingers to find any rough spots. It should *look* and *feel* smooth. Be patient and don't try to hurry the job. Hardly anyone really enjoys sanding, although everyone admires a smoothly finished surface when the work is finally done.

Now you are ready for finishing your cheese board. You will want to leave the wood natural, with only a coat of vegetable oil to protect it and to bring out the grain (see Part II, page 104).

CHAPTER THREE

Gluing Things Together

The place where 2 pieces of wood are joined is called a *joint*. Glue is used to join and hold small pieces of wood together, and for a small project it is sufficient. For a large project you need nails, too, but glue will hold the pieces together while you hammer in the nails, and it will make the joint stronger.

USING GLUE

Sand the wood pieces that are to be glued together so they are clean and smooth.

Before you begin gluing, place one piece against the other and draw a light guideline on the wood to show where the glue is to be applied.

Put a thin layer of glue on both surfaces. If you apply too much, the glue will squeeze out messily between the 2 pieces when you press them together.

Professional woodworkers apply glue with a brush, but you can use your finger or a stick. Squeeze the glue directly from the bottle onto the wood and spread it.

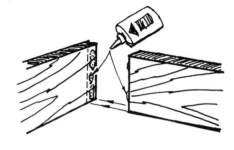

Then put the two glued surfaces together, making sure the edges line up evenly. Work quickly, because the glue sets fast. Press the pieces together hard.

With a damp cloth or sponge clean off *all* the excess glue that squeezes out, before it has a chance to dry. Let the pieces dry without disturbing them.

Professional woodworkers have an assortment of clamps for holding joints while they dry, but clamps are expensive and for· simple projects you can get along without them.

MAKING A CANDLESTICK

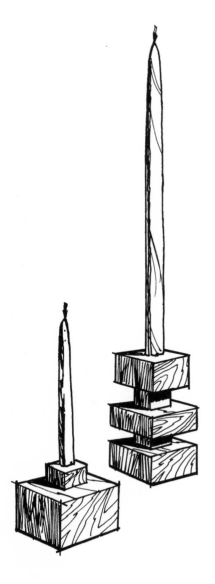

You can design and make an attractive candlestick by gluing together blocks of wood, one on top of the other. It can be as simple as you like. Just a single block of wood, nicely finished, makes a very handsome candlestick. Or make a rather elaborate candelabra for holding several candles. A common nail glued to the top block with epoxy glue is the spike that holds the candle.

Your choice of design probably will depend on what kind of wood you have to work with. If you have some small blocks of different shapes and sizes, try arranging them in various ways. You can put smaller blocks between larger ones or have each block smaller than the one below it. The biggest block should be on the bottom, so that the candlestick doesn't topple over. The top block should extend at least 1″ beyond the circumference of the candle you plan to use.

A pillar candle about 1½″ thick, which comes with a hole drilled up through the bottom, is the best for this kind of candlestick.

If you don't have any blocks of wood that seem right to you, cut up some scraps of lumber or even plywood and make your own blocks. If the wood is thin, cut several pieces the same size and glue them together to form a block—somewhat like the way plywood is made.

First, remember to square the end of the board. Mark the cutting line. Clamp the board and saw it.

Put together as many layers as you want to make a "sandwich." Be sure the edges are even when you glue the pieces.

Make several blocks this way, of different shapes and sizes. Sand the blocks well before you glue them together.

Now center each block on the one to which it is to be glued, using a small ruler to check the measurements. Draw a few guidelines very lightly around the smaller block on the surface of the larger block.

To keep the blocks from getting mixed up, mark the sides that are going to be glued together with identical letters or numbers.

Glue a smaller block to a larger one. Be sure to clean off the excess glue that squeezes out. Put together only 2 blocks at a time, and let them dry for about an hour. Then glue the sections together.

Before you put the candle spike on the top, finish the candlestick in one of the ways suggested in Part II. If the wood is especially attractive and you want to keep its natural appearance, simply wipe on a prepared oil finish to bring out its beauty (page 104).

Or, if you like the grain of the wood but want to darken it to look like mahogany or walnut, for example, stain it (page 106). Then protect it with a prepared oil finish (page 104) or varnish (page 109).

If you made the blocks with pieces of plywood, you can hide the unattractive edges by painting the candlestick (page 111). For a special touch, glaze it after it has been painted (page 121).

When the candlestick is completely dry, mark the exact center of the top block. Use an epoxy glue to fasten the head of a 2″ common nail to the top block for the spike.

Epoxy glue comes in 2 separate tubes of ingredients. When equal amounts of each are mixed together, they react chemically to form an extremely strong glue.

Squeeze a small amount from each tube into a jar lid or onto a piece of paper or scrap of wood. Mix the ingredients with a toothpick, bit of wood, or nail.

Be careful not to get the glue on anything or you will not be able to clean it off. Try not to get any on your skin, but if you do, wash it off immediately with soap and water. Dip the head of the nail in the epoxy and center it on the mark on the wood.

If you don't have epoxy glue, try a white glue or some other glue made for handcrafts. Neither is as strong as epoxy, and the weight of the candle may break off the nail. You can replace it, of course, but you should not light the candle until you are sure it is held firmly in place.

If the candle you are planning to use doesn't have a hole already pierced through the bottom you can make one with an awl or a long common nail. Push the nail through a piece of cork or some other material (even a piece of carrot or potato), to serve as a "handle," that will not catch fire or get hot.

Hold the point of the awl or nail in the flame of a lighted candle or over the burner of the kitchen stove for a few seconds. Don't touch the metal—it will burn you. Then push the point into the bottom of the candle next to the wick. Repeat this operation several times until you have pierced a hole about 2″ deep into which the nail spike will fit. (You may need an older person to help you make the hole.)

MAKING A TRAY

With a piece of wood and some strips of decorative molding you can make a practical tray for carrying food and drinks.

The size of the tray will depend on what it will be used for. If you want to serve someone breakfast in bed, for instance, lay out lengthwise on a newspaper all the things that you would put on the tray and draw a rectangle around them, allowing a few extra inches on each side.

A tray 14″ x 21″ should be large enough for serving breakfast. If it is much larger, it will be hard to handle. You will need ¼″ or ½″ plywood or hardboard, like Masonite.

The molding is to provide an edge to keep things from sliding off the tray. There are many different kinds of molding, ranging from plain rounded to very fancy carved strips. Whatever style you choose, the width ideally should be no more than ¾″. If you don't have molding, you can cut narrow strips of wood.

You will need enough to go around all 4 sides of the tray. Molding is sold in lumberyards in lengths of 2′, 3′, and 4′. Two 3′ lengths would be perfect. Measure and cut a 14″ piece and a 21″ piece from each 3′ length.

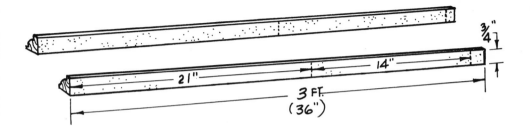

CUTTING A MITERED CORNER

When you lay the strips on top of the board along the edges, you'll find that the ends overlap. One way to arrange them is to cut two of the pieces a little shorter so that they meet but no longer overlap.

A better way is to miter the corners by cutting each strip of molding at a 45-degree angle. Mitered corners are cut most accurately with the help of a miter box. But you can, if you're careful, do a nice job using only a board as a guide.

Find a board at least 4½" wide—wider, if possible—and about 2' long. Square the end of the board.

Measure the width of the board *exactly*. Then measure that same amount from the end of the board. For example, if the board is 4⅝" wide, measure exactly 4⅝" from the end and draw a line across the board. You will have a perfect square.

Then draw diagonal lines from each end of the line to the opposite corners of the board. Make the same markings on the opposite end of the board. Draw a line down the center of the board that goes right through the center points where the diagonal lines cross.

Lay the molding strip on the board with the edge away from you against the long center line. The corner of the end that you are going to cut should just touch the

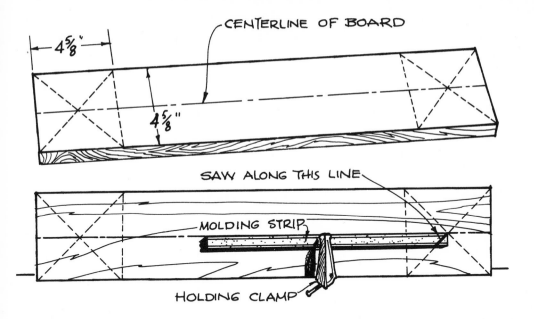

CENTERLINE OF BOARD

$4\frac{5}{8}$"

$4\frac{5}{8}$"

SAW ALONG THIS LINE

MOLDING STRIP

HOLDING CLAMP

center point. The diagonal will be your cutting line for an angled end that will perfectly fit the angled end of the strip it meets.

Clamp both the strip and the board flat along the edge of your worktable.

Line up the saw with the diagonal line that goes under the end of the molding strip. Keep the saw level instead of slanted, and saw back and forth through the molding. Keep your eye on the line as you cut. Saw down to the board but not into it.

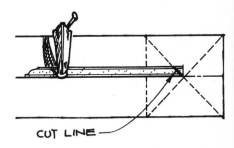

CUT LINE

To cut the opposite end, turn the strip around and lay it on the board with the edge toward you against the long center line. The corner should just touch the center point. Saw through the molding.

Lay the mitered strips on the board for the tray and check them for fit. It the corners don't join smoothly, sand them or fill in the gaps later with wood putty. Before you glue on the strips, sand all the parts.

Lay the molding strips on the board and lightly sketch a guideline for gluing. Then spread the glue along one edge of the board and on one piece of molding and put it in place. Repeat for each piece. Remember to put glue on the cut ends of each strip as you add it. Let the glue dry.

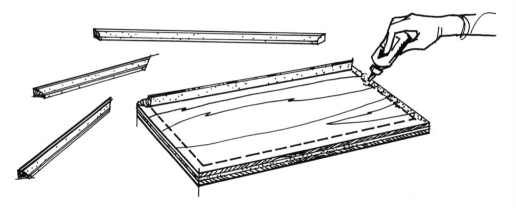

A tray is a perfect object for decoupage. First, paint the tray, following the directions on page 111. Paint the bottom and sides first. When it is dry enough to turn over, paint the inside and the molding. Give it a second coat.

After the paint is thoroughly dry, apply the decoupage cutouts (see page 123). Fruit and vegetable designs are especially suitable for a tray.

CHAPTER FOUR

Nailing Things Together

When you are joining large pieces of wood, or small pieces that will be handled a lot, glue is not strong enough to hold them firmly. The joint will be much stronger if you use nails.

Cartoonists often joke about clumsy people hitting thumbs, instead of nails, with a hammer. But if you start a nail the right way, there is no danger of hitting your thumb or anything else but the nail. For practice, use common nails with flat heads.

DRIVING NAILS

First, mark the exact spot where the nail is to go on a piece of wood that is thicker than the length of the nail. Push the point of an awl or the nail itself into the wood and twist it back and forth. This notch in the wood, called a *pilot hole,* helps to keep the nail from slipping.

Now hold the shank of the nail—the part below the head—between the thumb and index finger of your left hand (if you are right-handed). Hold the hammer halfway toward the head and gently tap it on the

nail. Tap just enough to get the point imbedded in the wood far enough so the nail will stand up by itself.

Now you're ready to drive the nail all the way into the wood. Hold the hammer near the end of the handle. Line up the face of the hammer with the head of the nail. Move your arm only from the elbow down and hit the nail on the head. Don't swing your whole arm. Let the weight of the hammer do the work.

If you hit the nail squarely, it will go straight into the wood. If you hit it at an angle, the nail will bend. Hit it until you get the head down to the surface of the wood.

Driving a nail is a skill that requires practice. Soon you'll be able to drive it all the way in with only a few hammer blows, and it will almost always go in straight.

But even experienced woodworkers sometimes bend a nail or put one where it doesn't belong. The forked end of a claw hammer is used to pull out a nail.

Hold the hammer upside down and slide the notch of the fork under the head of the nail. Place a piece of cardboard—an empty matchbook cover, for instance—under the hammer head to protect the wood. Then pull on the handle of the hammer so that the claws lift out the nail.

If the nail is a long one and extends a distance above the surface, you may have to put a block of wood under the head of the hammer to raise it high enough so the notch will grasp the nailhead.

MAKING A HOUSE NUMBER SIGN WITH NAILS

Using nails to make the numbers of a sign for your house is an interesting project that gives plenty of practice in driving nails. You can simply outline the numerals with nails or fill in the numerals as well.

Find a board at least 1″ thick and cut it to the size you want. If you are putting the sign near your front door or the driveway, you will want to make the numbers large enough so that they can be seen easily from a distance. If it will be attached on an apartment door, the numbers and the sign can be smaller. For a house, a sign 6″ x 6″ with the numerals 5″ high is suitable. For an apartment, a sign 4″ x 4″ with the numerals 3″ high is large enough. Make the sign wider if the house number is a long one. Use a piece of wood about 1″ x 12″ as a stake for holding the sign outdoors.

Sand the board. Stain it a dark color (see page 106). Finish with a plain outdoor varnish (see page 109). A painted surface may be damaged when you hammer in the nails.

Draw the numbers freehand on the board or use a stencil.

Use rustproof aluminum or galvanized-steel nails shorter than the thickness of the board.

Drive nails all along the outlines of the numbers as close together as you can, if possible with the heads touching but not overlapping. Then, if you want, you can fill in the outlines with more nails.

Nail the 12″ stake to the back of the sign, and pound the end of it into the ground.

To hang the sign on an apartment door, use adhesive-backed hooks and eyelets (follow directions on the package).

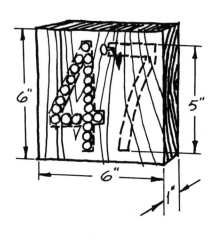

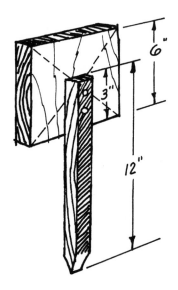

TOEING NAILS

Driving a nail in at a slight angle, rather than straight down, is called *toeing* the nail.

If you join two pieces of wood with slightly toed nails, the joint will be stronger.

To drive a nail at an angle without bending it, you must still hit the nail squarely on the head. Hammer in the direction the nail shank points. This means you must hold your arm at a slightly different angle when you pound.

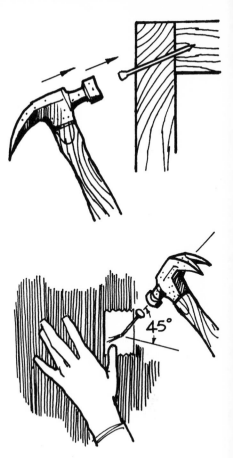

When you hammer a nail into a plaster wall to hang a picture, put a small piece of tape on the spot where the nail will go. This helps to keep the plaster from chipping. Use a finishing nail about 1½″ long. Holding the nail at a 45-degree angle, tap gently to get it started. Then drive it in to the last ½″.

If you are using a picture hook that comes with its own nail, your job is much easier, since the hook holds the nail at the correct angle. Just hold the hook in place against the wall and hammer the nail through the hook as far as it will go.

MAKING AN ASSEMBLAGE WITH NAILS

Artists are always looking for new materials to work with, and some have discovered the humble nail. They create works of art using different kinds of nails, driven only partway into the wood, to form interesting patterns and textures.

If you want to use nails as an art material, cut a board the size and shape you
want. Coat the wood with a prepared oil
finish to improve its natural appearance
(see page 104). Or stain it with a light
wood tone or a bright color (see page 106).

Sketch a design on the board and fill it
in with nails hammered only partway into
the wood. Start at the center of each section

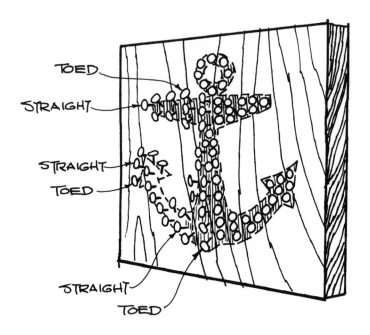

and hammer the nails in straight. As you
move toward the outlines of each section,
begin to toe the nails slightly. For contrast,
leave some parts empty or hammer the
nails in farther.

It's great fun—and it's also good practice.

MAKING A BUTT JOINT

There are many different kinds of joints —the places where two pieces of wood are joined. Some are used when extra strength is needed. Others are used when the joint is to be hidden, or when it is to be part of the design itself. Most of these joints require precise cutting and fitting with special tools.

The butt joint, in which one piece meets the other in a straight line, is the simplest. The parts in most of the projects in this book are joined with a butt joint.

You need to keep in mind how this joint is made when you're planning your work and deciding how to measure and cut each piece.

USING A WORKING DRAWING
AND A BILL OF MATERIALS

As the projects become more complicated, you'll find it much easier to write the details down on paper rather than to keep them in your head. A few simple drawings will show you how each part is to be cut and how the parts are to be joined. A *bill of materials* is a list of items that you need.

A bill of materials is given for each project. But if you decide to make something different or to change a project just a little, you should make up your own set.

First, on a plain piece of paper, draw a rough sketch called a *perspective* of the object you want to make. Draw it as though you were looking at it from an angle and could see the top and two sides. It doesn't have to be accurate. Then label each part "top," "back," "front," and so on. Remember to include the parts that don't show in the drawing. Point an arrow to show where they would be.

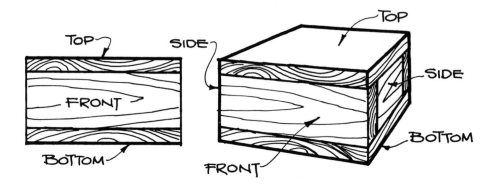

Next, list the parts and write down the dimensions of each. When you're figuring dimensions, always keep in mind the *actual* thickness of the wood you're using. You'll learn that sometimes you will have to add this thickness to the size of the piece, and sometimes you will have to subtract it.

Add to the list everything you will need besides the pieces of wood. In elaborate projects, you'll have such items as hinges and fasteners. This is your bill of materials. Nails, screws, and glue are not usually included in a bill of materials, but adding them might help you.

Then make your working drawings. If you have 2 or more parts the same size, you need draw only one. Label each part and mark the dimensions. You can use graph paper, and each $\frac{1}{4}''$ square can represent $1''$ of the actual dimensions.

If you don't have any graph paper, you can make some with a ruler and a piece of plain paper. Starting at the top edge, make a row of marks exactly $\frac{1}{4}''$ apart. Make a second row a few inches below the first one. Draw lines from top to bottom, using each pair of marks as a guide. In the same way, mark and draw lines from side to side.

But if you'd rather not go to all the trouble of making your own graph paper, you can make a drawing that is accurate enough, using just a ruler. Let $\frac{1}{4}''$ on the ruler equal $1''$ of the actual dimensions.

When you have all the materials you need, you're ready to begin measuring and marking.

LAYING OUT YOUR WORK

Cut out pieces of paper the size and shape of the parts you will need (newspaper is fine). Arrange the pieces on the lumber to show you where to mark and saw. Be sure to stay away from any knotholes or cracks.

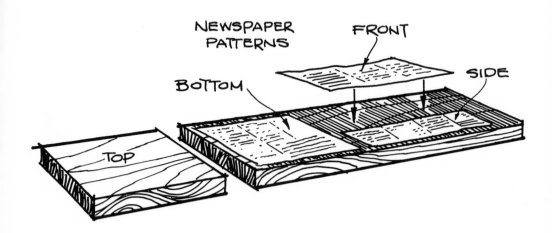

NEWSPAPER PATTERNS

FRONT

BOTTOM

SIDE

TOP

Cut the largest part first. Then see which smaller parts you can cut from what is left of the lumber. Because you should saw all the way across the wood, and not just cut out corners, mark the board where each major crosscut will be and fit the pieces of paper in between.

MAKING A FIVE-SIDED CUBE

An open box with 5 equal sides is a fine project for any woodworker. Cubes can be made in any size and used for many purposes. You could begin with a 6″ cube that can serve as a planter to hold a container in which a plant is growing.

This perspective shows how the cube will look and from it you can make up your drawings and bill of materials.

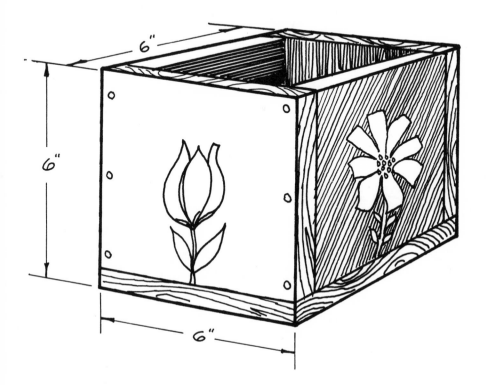

They may differ slightly from the ones shown here, depending on the thickness of the wood you use. And they will differ a lot if you decide to make a different-sized cube.

When you are constructing a box with butt joints, the usual method is to have the front and back pieces *overlap* the two side pieces. This means that the side pieces are cut shorter than the front and back.

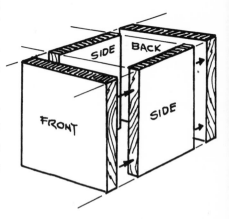

The bottom of the box can be .made in two ways. In Method I you join the 4 sides of the box and then nail on the bottom piece. This is the easier way, but the edges of the bottom piece will show unless you paint the box.

In Method II the 4 sides are joined around the bottom piece so that the edges of the piece are hidden. This method is a little more complicated, but the box is more attractive.

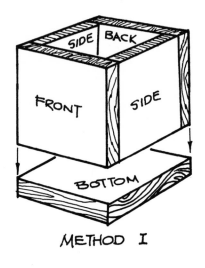

METHOD I

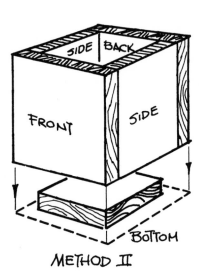

METHOD II

Decide which method you are going to use before you make your drawings and bill of materials. Both ways of making a 6″ x 6″ x 6″ cube, using wood ½″ thick, are shown.

Method I

The bottom is the only piece that measures a full 6″ x 6″.

Since the cube is to be 6″ high, each of the other pieces must be cut ½″ shorter than 6″ to allow for the thickness of the bottom. Each will be 5½″ high.

The front and back are each 6″ wide. From the width of each side piece you must subtract ½″ to allow for the thickness of the front piece and another ½″ to allow for the thickness of the back piece. The 2 sides for this cube, therefore, will each measure 5″ wide by 5½″ high.

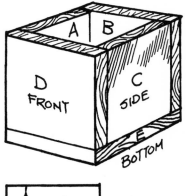

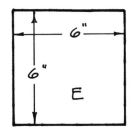
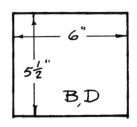
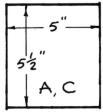

Your bill of materials will look like this:

Bill of Materials

NUMBER OF PIECES	PART AND USE	DIMENSIONS
1	E, bottom	6″ x 6″
2	B, front; D, back	6″ x 5½″
2	A and C, sides	5″ x 5½″

Lay out your work. Then measure, mark,

and cut one piece at a time. Be sure to check for squareness. Sand each part on both sides and along the edges. Lightly mark the name of the part on the wrong side of each piece.

Putting It Together

You are going to drive the nails all the way through the long pieces and into the ends of the short pieces. Use finishing nails at least twice as long as the thickness of the wood. If you are using $\frac{1}{2}''$ wood, the nails should be about $1''$ long.

To make sure the nails go in at the right place—not too close to the edge, but not too far away from it—use a ruler to measure and an awl or nail to mark where each nail is to go. Measure $\frac{1}{4}''$ from the edge of $\frac{1}{2}''$ wood. On the front, mark 3 holes for each of the 2 pieces to be joined to it.

Drive the nails all the way through the

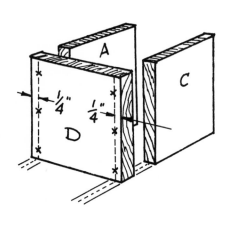
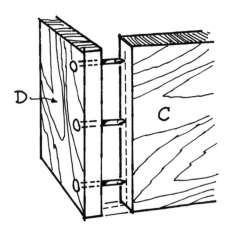

front piece until the tips come through on the other side.

Line up the end of one of the side pieces against the nails on the inside of the front piece. Press them together hard enough so that the tips of the nails make holes in the end of the wood.

Spread glue on the 2 surfaces to be joined. Press them together, with the nail tips in the holes. Then drive the nails in.

Before the glue sets, use the try square to check the corner for squareness. Fit the corner inside the angle of the try square and make sure the legs of the square line up exactly with both pieces. If necessary, you can bend the joint a little to make it square.

When the joints are dry, nail on the bottom piece. Drive 3 nails along each side. Press the bottom and sides together. Spread glue on the surfaces to be joined. Put them together again and drive the nails in.

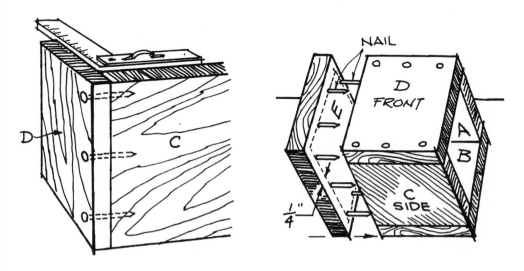

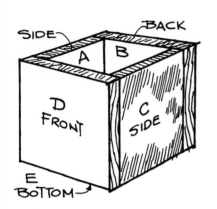

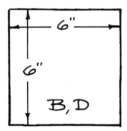

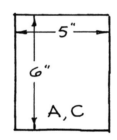

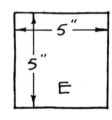

Method II

The front and back pieces measure a full 6″ x 6″. The side pieces are the same height, but from the width of each you must subtract ½″ to allow for the thickness of the front piece and another ½″ to allow for the thickness of the back piece. The 2 sides for this cube, then, will each measure 5″ wide by 6″ high.

The bottom, which fits inside the 4 pieces, will be ½″ less on each of its 4 edges. It will measure 5″ x 5″. Your bill of materials will look like this:

Bill of Materials

NUMBER OF PIECES	PART AND USE	DIMENSIONS
2	B, front; D, back	6″ x 6″
2	A and C, sides	5″ x 6″
1	E, bottom	5″ x 5″

Lay out your work. Then measure, mark, and cut one piece at a time. Be sure to check for squareness. Sand each part on

both sides and along the edges. Lightly
mark the name of the part on the wrong
side of each piece.

Putting It Together

You are going to drive nails all the way
through the long pieces and into the ends
of the short pieces. Use finishing nails at
least twice as long as the thickness of the
wood. If you are using ½″ wood, the nails
should be about 1″ long.

To make sure the nails go in at the right
place—not too close to the edge, but not too
far away from it—use a ruler to measure
and an awl or nail to mark where each is to
go. Measure ¼″ from the edge of ½″ wood.
On the bottom edges of the side pieces,
mark 3 holes where the bottom piece will
be joined to them.

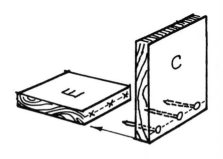

Drive the nails all the way through the
side pieces until the tips come through on
the other side.

Line up the bottom against the nails on
the inside of one of the side pieces. Press
them together hard enough so that the tips
of the nails make holes in the bottom.

Then spread glue on the 2 surfaces to
be joined. Press them together, with the
nail tips placed in the holes. Then drive the
nails in.

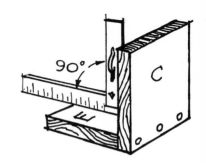

Before the glue sets, check the corner for
squareness with a try square. Fit the corner
inside the angle of the try square and make

sure the legs of the square line up exactly with both pieces. If necessary, you can bend the joint a little to make it square.

After the 2 sides have been glued and nailed, glue and nail the front piece to the edges of the bottom and 2 sides.

Glue and nail on the back piece.

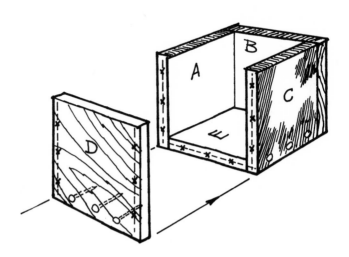

COUNTERSINKING NAILS

Unless you are going to paint the cube, you should countersink the nails so they don't show.

Use a nail set or another nail to drive the tops of the nails below the surface of the wood. Put the pointed end of the nail set on the head of the nail. Rest your hand against the wood and keep the nail set straight. Tap it with a hammer until the

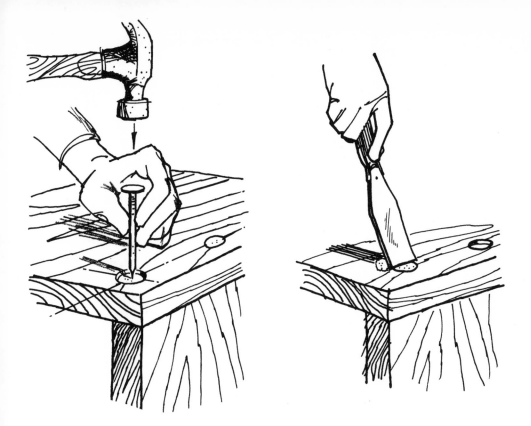

top of the nail is sunk about $\frac{1}{8}''$ below the surface.

Then, with a putty knife, fill the hole with wood putty. Use your thumb or the knife to push the putty into the hole.

Use the knife to scrape away any excess and to even off the top.

You can paint the cube or, if the wood is especially nice, finish it naturally or stain it and then varnish it. Consider painting the inside of the planter a dark color (to help hide the container) and the outside and top edge a bright color.

You could also stencil a flower design on each side of the planter.

But before you begin to finish the wood, turn to Part II, page 100, and learn how to get the surface ready for finishing. Then choose the kind of finish you want.

MAKING A TEN-INCH CUBE

Once you've mastered the construction of the cube, you have the necessary techniques to try many interesting projects. For example, a 10″ cube, open side up, can be used as a wastebasket. Turn it over and it

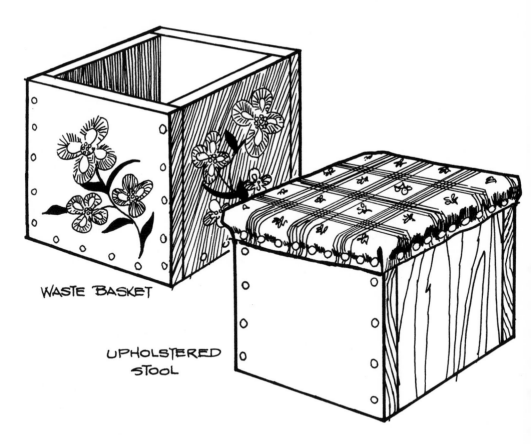

WASTE BASKET

UPHOLSTERED
STOOL

becomes a seat. (Use either Method I or
II to make the wastebasket, but the cube
made by Method I is stronger for the seat.)
You can upholster the top with a piece of
fabric or even fancy needlework after you
have finished the 4 sides.

Here are bills of materials for a 10″ cube
made by both methods, using ½″ stock.

Method I
Bill of Materials

NUMBER OF PIECES	PART AND USE	DIMENSIONS
1	E, bottom	10″ x 10″
2	B, front; D, back	10″ x 9½″
2	A and C, sides	9″ x 9½″

Method II
Bill of Materials

NUMBER OF PIECES	PART AND USE	DIMENSIONS
2	B, front; D, back	10″ x 10″
2	A and C, sides	9″ x 10″
1	E, bottom	9″ x 9″

If you are making a wastebasket, you
could stain it in a wood tone and then use
a prepared oil finish. Or you could paint it
and decorate one side with a decoupage design that blends with the room in which it
will be used or that reflects the interests of
the person who will be using it—music or
animals or sports, for example.

If you are making a seat, stain it in a
dark wood tone (you don't need to stain

the inside) and varnish it or use a prepared oil finish. Then upholster the top if you like.

Before you begin to finish the wood, turn to Part II, page 100, and learn how to get the surface ready for finishing. Then choose the kind of finish you want to use.

UPHOLSTERING A SEAT

Cut a piece of foam rubber sheet 1″ wider and 1″ longer than the top (11″ for a 10″ cube). If you don't have any foam, you can use an old blanket several layers thick. (Make sure it's an *old* blanket and that you have permission to use it.) Use dabs of glue to hold the padding in place. Glue the edges down over the edges of the cube. Cut a small wedge out of each corner to make a smooth fit.

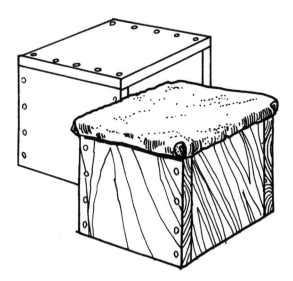

The fabric or needlework should measure about 2″ wider and longer than the top (12″ x 12″ for a 10″ cube).

Fold under the raw edges just enough so the folded edge hides the joint where the top meets the sides. Fasten the fabric with upholstery nails or other roundheaded nails. If you don't have either, use common nails. (Finishing nails will slip through the fabric.) Hammer only a few along one side, just enough to hold the fabric in place. Leave the corners free. Fasten the opposite side next. Keep the top smooth; don't pull it too tightly. Then nail down the 2 remaining sides.

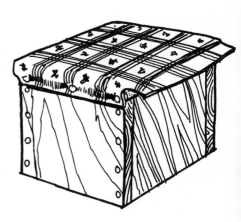

Now go back and put nails all the way around, about ½″ apart. When you come to the corners, make little folds or pleats as neatly as you can to take up the fullness.

MAKING A SIXTEEN-INCH CUBE

Here are bills of materials for a 16″ cube, made by both methods, using ¾″ plywood.

Method I
Bill of Materials

NUMBER OF PIECES	PART AND USE	DIMENSIONS
1	E, bottom	16″ x 16″
2	B, front; D, back	16″ x 15¼″
2	A and C, sides	14½″ x 15¼″

Method II
Bill of Materials

NUMBER OF PIECES	PART AND USE	DIMENSIONS
2	B, front; D, back	16″ x 16″
2	A and C, sides	14½″ x 16″
1	E, bottom	14½″ x 14½″

A 16″ cube is the size used for storing phonograph records. If you build several cubes, they can be stacked to make a storage wall for books or other treasures as well as for records. Coat them with some of the bright-colored stains—one red, one yellow, a third blue—then varnish.

Painted in gay colors, cubes make good toy bins for younger children in your family. When decorated with decoupage pictures, they will help remind preschoolers which toys go where.

Turned upside down, the 16″ cube makes a convenient snack table. (Use Method I for building it.) Stain it in a dark wood tone and use a prepared oil finish, or paint it shiny black or another color. With a bright cushion on top—or without one—it's an extra seat.

Before you begin finishing, turn to Part II, page 100, and learn how to get the surface ready.

PUTTING A LID ON THE CUBE

The list of possibilities for cubes grows even longer when you add a lid. Then a cube becomes a box for keeping private things, like letters, seashells, buttons, or whatever you have that needs its own special place.

One way to add a lid is simply to cut the sixth side of the cube. Then, to keep the lid from sliding off, glue to its underside a second, smaller piece that will fit inside the box.

For a 6″ cube made of ½″-thick wood, cut a 6″ x 6″ piece for the lid. Make the inside piece just a little *less* than 5″ x 5″ so that it doesn't fit too tightly.

On the wrong side of the larger piece, measure ½″ in from each edge and draw guidelines for gluing. Glue the 2 pieces together.

If you wish, you can glue a wooden knob in the center of the top.

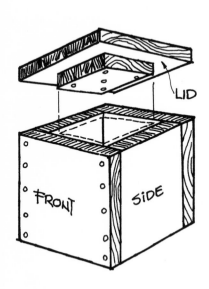

USING HINGES

Another way to add a lid is to attach it with hinges. Hardware stores and some craft-supply stores sell decorative hinges for boxes of all sizes. They come with their own little roundheaded ornamental nails called *escutcheon pins*. (Originally an escutcheon was a shield, which was part of a knight's armor, and one of its meanings today is a metal piece that ornaments and protects wood.)

You should use solid wood for the lid,

rather than plywood, even if you have made the box of plywood. The reason is that escutcheon pins will hold better in solid wood than they will in the layered edge of plywood. The difference in woods won't be obvious if you paint the cube.

Put the hinges on *after* you have finished the box and lid. Turn to Part II, page 100, to find out how to prepare the surface before you begin finishing. Try painting the box in two colors. For example, paint the inside dark blue and the outside bright green (or the other way around). The edges where the lid and box come together should be painted the same color as the outside.

The hinges should be placed about a quarter of the box length in from each end. If you are hinging a 6″ box, you would put the hinges about 1½″ from each end.

Place the hinges so that the barrel—the joining of the two parts of the hinge—is centered over the seam where the lid and the box come together. Use a sharp pencil to mark through the holes in the hinge for the pins.

Lay the hinges aside and make pilot holes. Put each hinge back in place with the hinge holes centered over the pilot holes. Hammer in the pins.

You might also want a catch for keeping the box closed. Attach it to the center front of the box the same way you attached the hinges.

If you have built a small box out of thin wood, you can make a hinge with strips of cloth tape, like Mystic tape, or even with strong closely woven fabric and glue. After you have finished the box and lid, cut 2 strips of tape or fabric the length of the lid —one for the inside, the other for the outside. The strips should be about twice as wide as the thickness of the wood.

Fold one strip of tape in half lengthwise, sticky side out. Lay the tape along one edge of the box, with the fold along the outside edge of the wood. Or coat one side of the fabric with glue and put it on the same way.

Put the lid on and press the tape in place on the inside of the lid. With the lid firmly closed, put the second piece of tape, folded in half lengthwise, on the outside of the box with the fold along the edge.

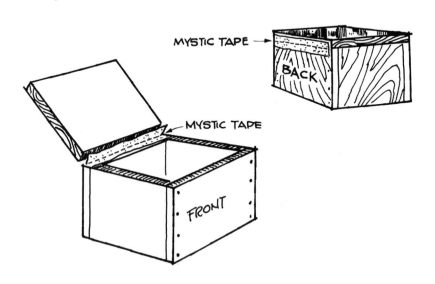

MAKING A SEWING BOX

A sewing box—or jewelry box or a box for hobby or craft supplies—can be constructed with a simple hinged top. Carefully finished outside and imaginatively fitted out inside, it makes a fine gift. You'll probably want one yourself.

First decide on its use, and then on the shape and size. You might find that a shape other than a cube is more suited to the use you have in mind. A convenient size for a sewing box is 8″ wide by 10″ long by 6″ high. A jewelry box can be smaller, but a toolbox should be larger. You can also make a second, shallow box (this one without a lid) to fit inside the large one.

If you plan to make the box 8″ x 10″ x 6″ H (*H* stands for high) with ½″ thick wood, constructed by Method II, you can use the bill of materials given here. But remember that if you make one change, most of the other measurements will change too. Then you must prepare your own bill of materials and working drawings.

Bill of Materials

NUMBER OF PIECES	PART AND USE	DIMENSIONS
2	A, front; B, back	6″ x 10″
2	C and D, sides	6″ x 7″
1	E, lid	8″ x 10″
1	F, bottom	7″ x 9″
2	metal hinges with pins	no more than ¾″ wide

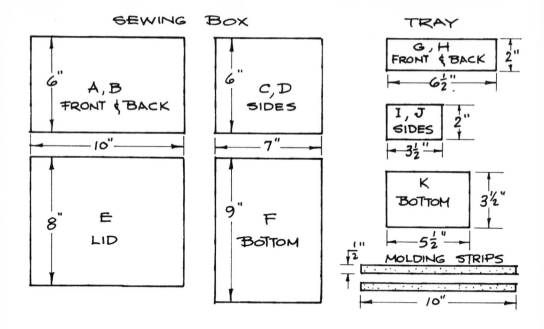

If you'd like to add a small tray to fit inside (which is very useful and much easier to make than it sounds), you'll need a second set of materials. Make the tray ½″ less than the inside width of the box and only half the inside length so that it will be easy to lift out and easy to slide on two strips of molding from one side to the other when you want to get at the items in the bottom. The tray would measure 4½″ x 6½″ x 2″ H.

Bill of Materials

NUMBER OF PIECES	PART AND USE	DIMENSIONS
2	G, front; H, back	2″ x 6½″
2	I, J, sides	2″ x 3½″
1	K, bottom	3½″ x 5½″
2	molding strips	8″ long and ½″ wide

Sand all the pieces. First, construct the box, using Method **II** (but don't put the lid on yet). Make the tray next.

The tray will rest on the molding strips, glued to the front and the back of the box. Put the strips in so that the top of the tray is about ½″ lower than the top of the box. For instance, if the tray is 2″ high, measure 2½″ from the top of the box on the inside of the front and the back. Draw a guideline. Center the strips *below* the guideline and glue them in place.

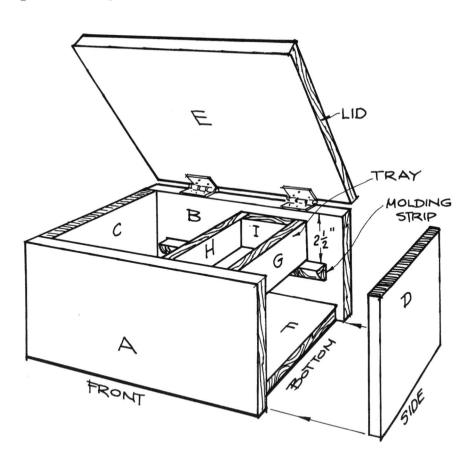

Countersink the nails and fill in the holes with wood putty. Choose a finish for the box suitable for its use and the kind of wood you used. First, turn to Part II, page 100, to find out how to prepare the surface for finishing. Then, for a sewing box, if the wood is attractive, give it a natural finish, varnishing the box and lid inside and out. Or stain it a dark wood tone or a bright color, then varnish it.

For a jewelry box, first paint the box and lid inside and out. You can stop at this point, or you can add a decorative finish: glaze the outside of the box; make a decoupage design on the lid; or stencil a monogram on it.

Then attach the lid to the box with hinges.

So that the lid can be kept open without falling back and damaging the hinges, it's a good idea to add a strap in each corner of the hinge. You can use strips of cloth, ribbon, braid, or rickrack for the straps.

Cut 2 pieces about 6" long. Glue one end of each piece about 3" above the hinged edge of the top. Place it a bit more than ½" in from the side edges, so the strap won't keep the lid from closing tightly.

Now open the lid and let it lean back just a little (beyond a straight-up position). Glue the other end of the straps on the inside of each side piece, about 3" from the hinged edge.

Use little nails to help fasten the straps in place.

Carrying handles are a great convenience for a sewing box. Cut a piece of heavy braid or webbing 3 times as long as the box. (For a 10″ box, it will be 30″ long.) Cut the piece in half.

Form a U-loop by folding each piece. Turn under ½″ or so of the ends to keep them from unraveling and nail the ends on the side of the box 3″ from the top, one end near the front and the other end near the back.

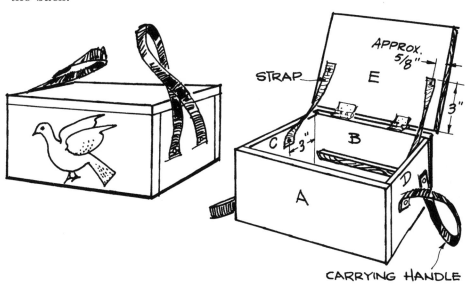

CARRYING HANDLE

PUTTING ANOTHER KIND OF LID ON A BOX

Another way to add a lid is to make a second box, which rests upside down over the first one. Both top and bottom boxes must be the same length and width, but the top can be much shallower than the bottom.

Use Method II to construct both parts. Finish them separately, then add the hinges and a catch, if you want one.

MAKING A CARD FILE

A wooden box made to hold 3″ x 5″ cards is used for filing many things—from addresses to recipes to a catalogue for books, records, or other collections. Make the bottom of the box wide enough to hold the cards but only deep enough so that you can read what is written on the tops of the cards as you flip through them. It can be as long as you want it, depending on how many cards will be kept in the file.

If you are using ½″ stock to make the

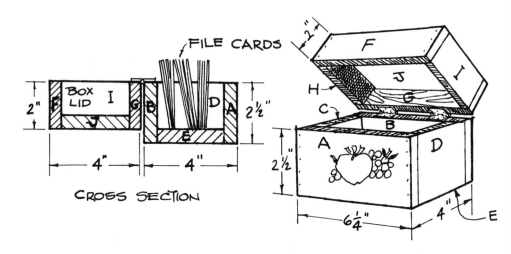

file, the outside measurements of the closed box might be 6¼″ x 4″ x 4½″ H (the bottom would be 2½″ H, the top 2″ H). Here is the bill of materials for a box of this size. Remember that if you change even one of the measurements, you will have to change at least some of the others.

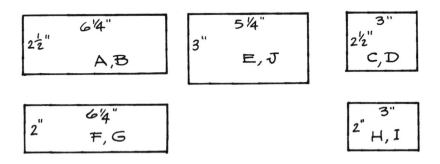

Bill of Materials

NUMBER OF PIECES	PART AND USE	DIMENSIONS
2	A, front; B, back	2½″ x 6¼″
2	C and D, sides	2½″ x 3″
2	F, lid front; G, lid back	2″ x 6¼″
2	H and I, lid sides	2″ x 3″
2	E, bottom; J, top	3″ x 5¼″

Construct the two boxes, using Method II for both. Turn to Part II, page 100, to find out how to prepare the surface for finishing. Stain the wood and varnish it. Or you can paint it. This is a fine decoupage project. Finish each box separately; then add the hinges.

MAKING A MINIATURE HOUSE

Most children enjoy playing with a miniature house. Girls like to use it as a doll-house, and boys often pretend it is a farm or a garage for their toy animals or cars. Almost any child you know would be delighted to have a make-believe toy house, and you certainly can have fun building and decorating one.

A miniature house is not much more complicated to make than a box, if you follow a simple plan. The bottom of the box is the front of the house, the long sides form the floor and ceiling, the 2 short sides form the walls, and the top of the box is left open. The house shown here is a good size to play with and easy for you to work with. To make it a different size, you will have to be very careful about changing the angle of the roof. (Ask someone who knows geometry to help you figure it out.) Use ¼″ hardboard, plywood, or paneling for the project.

Bill of Materials

NUMBER OF PIECES	PART AND USE	DIMENSIONS
2	A, ceiling; B, floor	9″ x 17″
3	C, D, and E, walls	8″ x 9″
1	F, roof section	10″ x 14″
1	G, roof section	10″ x 13¾″
1	H, front	17″ x 17″ (to be cut to shape later)

Lay out your work. Measure, mark, and cut each piece.

Cut section H, the front, so that it will follow the shape of the peak roof. Measure 8½″ from either end of the piece along 2 edges. Draw line x-y across the center of the board.

Then measure 8½″ along the other 2 edges and draw line z-z across the board. Draw a line connecting x-z and another line connecting y-z, which are your cutting lines. It is important to saw these lines accurately so that the roof will fit.

Sand just the edges.

Putting It Together

Now build the house just as though you were making a box, using Method I.

Parts A and B, the ceiling and floor, are the long sides of the box. Parts C, D, and E, the walls, are the short sides, with D an extra "side" in the middle. Measure 8½″ from the end of part A and part B so that you know where to fasten part D. Glue and nail the side and middle walls of the box.

Part H, the front of the house, is the bottom of the box. Glue and nail it in place. The peak, of course, will extend beyond the side of the box.

Now stand the box on part B, the floor, so that the peak of section H sticks straight up. The roof goes on last, attached to the sloping sides of section H.

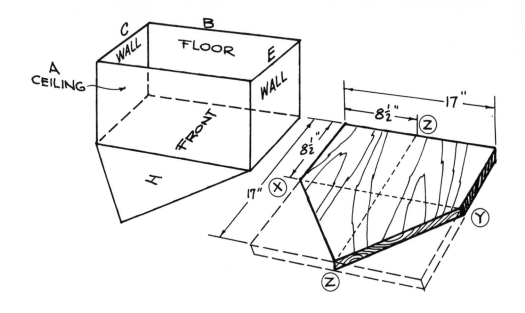

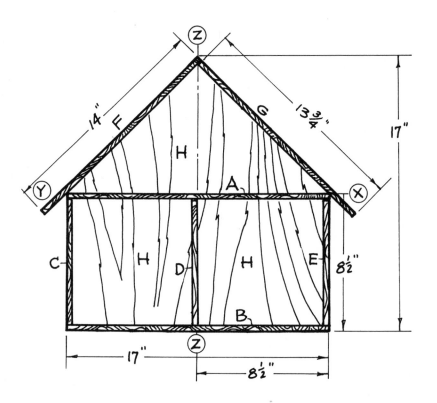

Glue and nail together the two roof sections F and G, making sure that the slightly shorter section G butts against the longer section F.

Then put the roof on so that it overhangs the front of the house, part H, by about ¾″ and is even with the open back of the house.

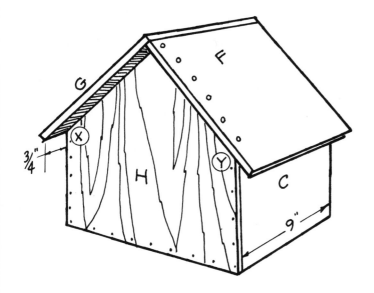

The roof is glued and nailed only to the front section, part H. It merely rests on the side walls, because the roof meets the walls at an angle and a joint would be too difficult to do well. There should be no problems with this construction if you remind the owner to carry the house holding it by the ceiling not by the roof.

The most enjoyable part of this project is the finishing and decorating. It's so much fun, in fact, that the child you're making it for probably will insist on helping you.

How you finish the house, of course, depends on what it is to be. If you have built it of wood paneling, you might not want to paint the outside of the house, except the roof. Countersink the nails and fill the holes with wood putty.

If it is a traditional doll's house, you will want to paint doors and windows on both the inside and the outside. Use a small brush to fill in the outlines that you draw first with a pencil. Or glue on cardboard or construction paper cutouts.

Use scraps of wood—both ¼″ board and thick blocks—to make furniture. Try to make it to scale, about 1″ to the foot. That means, if a real bed measures 6½′ in length, a bed for the doll's house would measure about 6½ *inches*.

Here are designs for some pieces. If you want to make others, you can measure the furniture in your own home and build the miniatures roughly to scale. Keep the construction simple.

Paint or glue on interesting details for realism. Use scraps of fabric to make rugs, curtains, bedspreads, and so on.

If the house is to be used as a barn, you might want to build separate stalls for the animals. You could put gates on the stalls with tiny hinges.

If it is to be a service station, you could decorate it with pictures of gasoline products cut from magazines. Paint little blocks of wood to look like gas pumps.

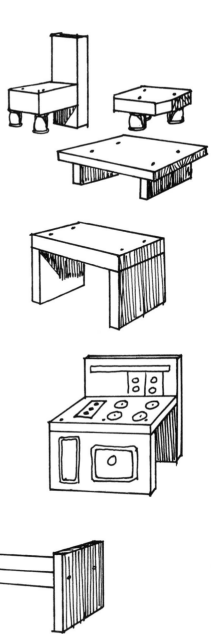

CHAPTER FIVE

Screwing Things Together

The larger the object, the more wear and tear it will get, the stronger the joints must be. Glue is all right for small, light projects. Nails are better for things like boxes. But screws are best for more complicated construction and for attaching sturdy hardware so that it won't work loose.

DRILLING SCREW HOLES

The right way to use screws is to drill holes with a hand drill in both pieces of wood where the screws are to go. If the wood is 1″ thick (actually ¾″), you should be using 2″ screws. You will drill all the way through the first piece of wood and just a little less than 1″ into the second piece. The screw slides through the first piece of wood and bites into the second piece as you turn it with a screwdriver.

First, nail the joint with two small finishing nails, one at each end. The nails will hold the joint while you drill the holes. Check the corner for squareness. If it isn't perfectly square, bend it until it is.

With a pencil, mark the place where the

screw will go and punch a pilot hole exactly on the mark.

A hand drill usually comes with bits of several sizes. Use a bit a little smaller than the thickness of the screw at the narrow end *inside* the grooves.

To change bits, hold the *chuck*—the textured metal piece at the bottom of the drill —in your right hand and turn the drill handle toward you. That opens the chuck and frees the bit. Put the new bit in place, hold the chuck firmly, and turn the drill handle forward to tighten the chuck.

Measure the length of the screw along the bit and put a piece of tape on the bit to mark off the length of the screw. That will show you how far to drill.

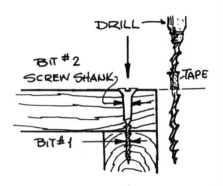

Rest the tip of the bit in the pilot hole. Be sure the drill is going straight down into the wood—not at an angle. Drill until the tape mark is even with the surface of the wood.

Then change to a bit that is the same thickness as the shank (the smooth part of the screw below the head). Redrill the hole, this time going only through the top piece of wood. If the wood is ¾″ thick, make a mark around the bit with tape ¾″ from the tip.

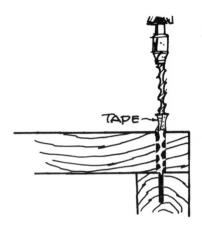

Drop the screw into the drilled hole. Use a screwdriver (be sure you have the right size) to drive the screw tightly into the second piece of wood.

Put the tip of the screwdriver firmly in the slot of the screw. Use some pressure as you turn the screwdriver, but don't press down too hard or the blade may slip and cut a gash in the wood, or—much worse—cut a gash in *you*. Always keep the screwdriver pointed *away* from you and keep your face out of the way.

Use both hands to turn the screwdriver, until the head of the screw is even with the surface of the wood. As the screw gets harder to turn, press harder on the screwdriver so it will stay in the slot.

MAKING A BENCH

You can make a strong, simple bench with only 3 pieces of wood and a few screws. The size of the bench depends on how it will be used and the wood you have.

A convenient size would be about 1′ wide (actually 11⅝″) by 3′ long by 1′ H. Of

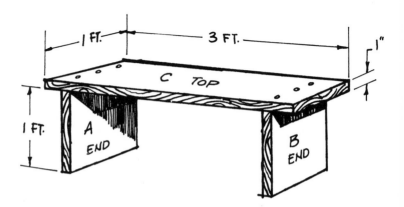

course, it can easily be made higher or longer (but not so easily made wider). It should be made of 1″ thick lumber (actually ¾″).

Bill of Materials

NUMBER OF PIECES	PART AND USE	DIMENSIONS
2	A and B, ends	11⅝″ x 12″
1	C, top	11⅝″ x 36″

Measure, mark, and cut the pieces. Don't forget to square each piece. Then sand them before you start to assemble the bench.

Set the end pieces, or "legs," in a few inches from the edges of the top. Measure and draw guidelines on the underside of the top, marking exactly where the end pieces will go.

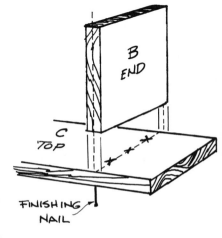

Glue and nail one end piece in place with 2 small finishing nails. Check the joint for squareness.

Use 3 2″ #8 wood screws. Measure to locate the spot through the center of the end piece where each screw will go, and mark it. If you plan to leave the bench unpainted, be sure the screws are evenly spaced. You don't have to be quite so careful if they will be hidden under a coat of paint. They should be about 3″ apart.

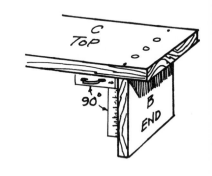

Punch pilot holes. Drill the holes, then redrill through the top board, using a larger bit.

Slide the screws into the holes and screw

them down tightly. Join the second end piece the same way.

Finish the bench, using one of the methods given in Part II, page 100.

MAKING A BOOKCASE

A bookcase is really just a box with shelves. Add a simple door to the box, and you have a cabinet. Constructing a drawer is a bit more complicated, but a drawer makes a simple bookcase or cabinet even more useful. The challenge is to have all the parts accurately cut and perfectly squared so that the door or drawer fits correctly. If you're really ambitious, you can try building 2 cabinets—one with a door, one with a drawer—and adding a top to make a desk or sewing table.

Decide on the size of the bookcase. If you are going to put a top on it to make a desk, it should be no more than 28″ high. The usual height for a desk or table is 29″. If you put a 1″ thick top on a 28″ base, the desk will be full height. You can make it lower, if that would be more comfortable.

Make the bookcase any width you want. For a bookcase 15″ wide, use 1″ x 12″ boards (actually ¾″ x 11⅝″) for the top, bottom, and sides. Cut the back from a sheet of ¼″ hardboard, such as Masonite.

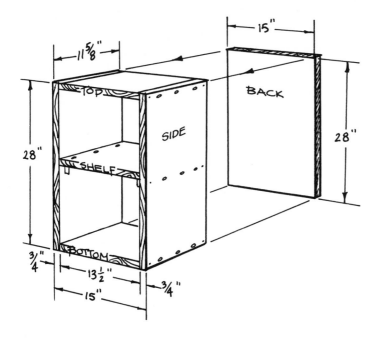

Here is a bill of materials for a bookcase 11⅝" x 15" x 28" H.

Bill of Materials

NUMBER OF PIECES	PART AND USE	DIMENSIONS
2	sides	11⅝" x 28"
3	top, bottom, shelf	11⅝" x 13½"
1	back	15" x 28"
2	molding strips	1" x 1" or ½" x 1", 10" long

Sand each piece before you begin to build the bookcase.

The shelf rests on molding strips fastened to each side of the bookcase. Where you place it will depend on the height of the books you want to shelve. Draw guidelines on the sides of the cabinet, making sure they match exactly, so the shelf will be level. Be sure the upper edge of the strip is placed along the guideline and is centered, leaving an inch on each side. Glue and nail the strips in place. You do not need to use screws.

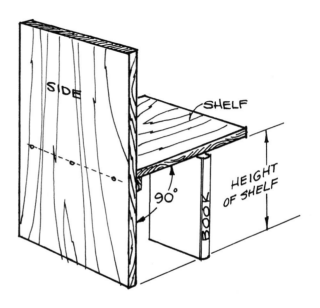

Put the bookcase together like a box, using Method I for construction.

Nail the first joint with 2 finishing nails. Check for squareness. Drill holes and drive in 3 screws. Make the second joint the same way.

Then nail the top and bottom and put screws in the joints.

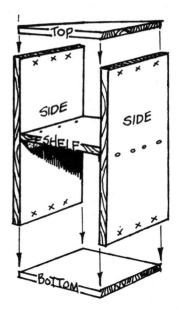

Put the shelf in place. To make it permanent, fasten the shelf to the molding strips with finishing nails.

Prepare the surface for finishing, following the directions in Part II, page 100. Then paint the bookcase, using 2 colors if you like. Or stain the wood and finish it with an oil preparation or with varnish.

UNDERSTANDING MORE ABOUT WORKING DRAWINGS

As woodworking projects become more complicated, the drawings also become more complicated. Then it is no longer enough to show only a perspective view or a front view. You must know what the object looks like from the top, the side, and the inside, as though it were cut in half.

For example, suppose you are planning to make a cabinet with a door and shelves. A perspective drawing shows you generally what the cabinet will look like from the outside.

Front view, top view, and side view show you a little more.

Working drawings based on these drawings show you how to measure and cut the outside pieces. But you still don't know how the inside is made.

For that you need a *section view,* as though the cabinet were cut in half like an

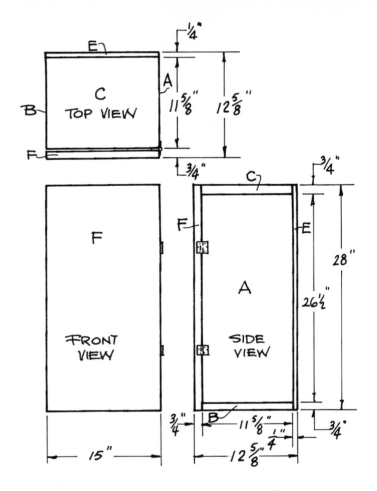

apple, down through the center from front to back. The hatched lines indicate wood that has been cut through. Where there are no hatched lines, you are looking at an uncut piece of wood.

In the section view of the cabinet shown here, you see a cross section of the door, top, bottom, back, and two shelves. But you also see 5 molding strips attached to the

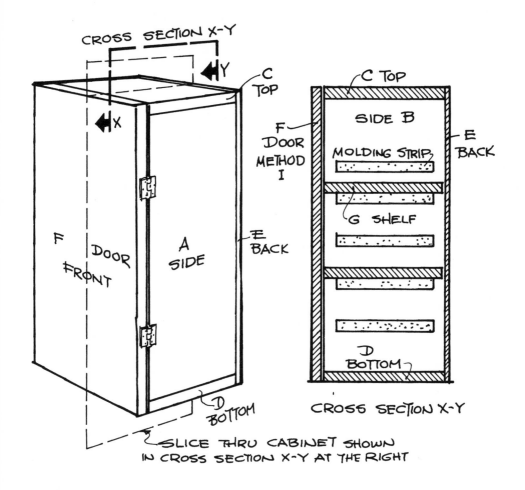

CROSS SECTION X-Y

C TOP

Y

C TOP

F DOOR METHOD I

SIDE B

E BACK

MOLDING STRIP

X

G SHELF

F DOOR FRONT

A SIDE

E BACK

E BACK

D BOTTOM

D BOTTOM

SLICE THRU CABINET SHOWN IN CROSS SECTION X-Y AT THE RIGHT

CROSS SECTION X-Y

side of the cabinet. They are not hatched, because they are not cut through.

It's more important for you to be able to understand section views than to draw them. Often when you are working on a project from someone else's plans, no directions are given in words. You make up your bill of materials and put the project together from drawings only.

MAKING A CABINET
WITH A DOOR

There are several ways to put a hinged door on a cabinet. You can cut a door that fits on the outside of the cabinet and covers all 4 edges. The hinge goes on the side of the cabinet. This is very much like making a cube by Method I. It's the simplest and is the kind that is described here.

Another way is to cut a door that fits just inside the 4 edges of the cabinet. Then the hinge is put on the front. This resembles a cube made by Method II, but it requires careful cutting and fitting.

In a third method, most commonly used in professional cabinetwork, the door fits half inside the edges but has a "lip" that overlaps the edges. The hinges are half or completely hidden. This technique requires special tools and know-how and will not be attempted in this book.

Here is a bill of materials for a cabinet that measures 12⅝" x 15" x 28" H with 2 removable shelves. It is made with 1" x 12" boards (actually ¾" x 11⅝"). The back is ¼" hardboard or plywood (you can use thicker plywood, if that's all you have). The door is ¾" plywood. You can also construct the entire cabinet of ¾" plywood, if you want to, and even off all the ⅝" measurements to a whole inch.

Bill of Materials

NUMBER OF PIECES	PART AND USE	DIMENSIONS
2	A and B, sides	$11\frac{5}{8}''$ x $26\frac{1}{2}''$
2	C and D, top and bottom	$11\frac{5}{8}''$ x $15''$
2	G and H, shelves	$11\frac{5}{8}''$ x $13\frac{1}{2}''$
1	E, back	$15''$ x $28''$
1	F, door	$15''$ x $28''$
2	leaf hinges	less than $1\frac{1}{2}''$ wide
1	catch	
2	molding strips	$1''$ x $1''$ or $\frac{1}{2}''$ x $1''$,
	(for each shelf position)	$10''$ long

The removable shelves rest on molding strips fastened to each side of the cabinet. To make adjustable shelves, fasten 2 or 3 extra strips on each side so that you can move the shelves higher or lower as needed.

Lay out your work. Then measure, mark, and cut each piece. Don't forget about squaring. Sand the pieces.

Attach the molding strips to the sides of the cabinet before you put the cabinet together. First, figure out where you want the shelves to be placed (the section view shows you one possibility), bearing in mind the height of the objects you plan to keep in the cabinet.

For instance, if you plan to keep a small microscope on the bottom shelf and you are making the cabinet of $\frac{3}{4}''$ wood, measure the height of the microscope, add an inch for clearance, plus $\frac{3}{4}''$ for the bottom

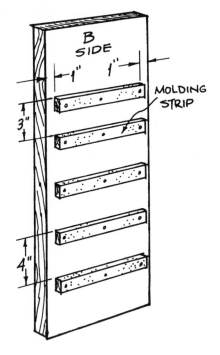

of the cabinet. Draw a guideline, then glue and nail a molding strip along the line. That strip will support the shelf above the microscope.

Attach each molding strip the same way. Measure very carefully to be sure the pairs of strips will be exactly opposite each other so the shelves will be level. (If you're planning to add a drawer, see page 94 to find out where to put the molding strips to hold the drawer.)

Then build the cabinet, using Method I. Notice, though, that the short ends of the box—actually the top and bottom of the cabinet—overlap the long sides, rather than the other way around. The bottom of the box, part E, has become the back of the cabinet and goes on last.

Make sure the shelves fit. If they are too tight, sand one edge.

HANGING THE DOOR

Before you attach the hardware, finish the door, the shelves, and the cabinet inside and out. See Part II, page 100, for instructions in preparing the surface for finishing. Then paint or stain it. If you stain it, finish it with an oil preparation or with varnish.

The hinges should be placed about a

quarter of the length from each end of
the door. For a door 28″ high, measure 7″
from each end for the hinge.

Place the barrel of the hinge along the
seam where the door meets the cabinet.
Use a sharp pencil to mark through the
holes in the hinge on the cabinet (not on
the door yet) where the screws will go.

Drill holes for the screws. Screw half
the hinge to the cabinet. Attach half of the
second hinge in the same way.

Then put the door in place, closed.
Through the holes in the other half of the
hinge mark the position on the edge of
the door.

Drill holes for the screws. Screw the
hinge to the door. Attach the second hinge.

Install a catch on the opposite edges of
the door and the cabinet, using the same
method.

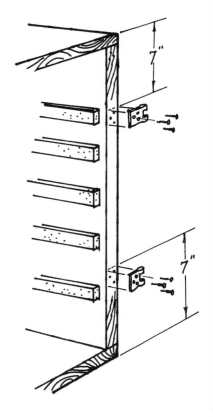

MAKING A DRAWER

A drawer should fit well and open and
close easily. It is really a small box without
a lid that slides inside a larger box.

The drawer shown here will fit in either
the cabinet or bookcase. It measures 10½″
x 13½″ at its widest point and will fit inside an 11⅝″ x 15″ cabinet or bookcase
built of ¾″ stock. It has no knob or pull,

but the front of the drawer is made with a lip at the top and bottom for pulling open.

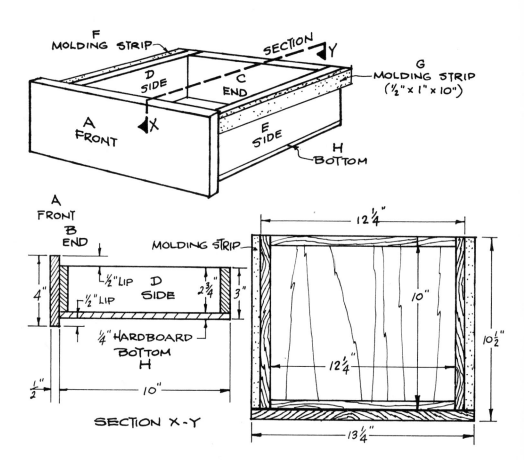

The molding strips along the sides of the drawer slide on molding strips nailed inside the cabinet. They hold the drawer in place and allow it to open and close smoothly.

Use ½″ stock, except ¼″ hardboard for bottom.

Bill of Materials

NUMBER OF PIECES	PART AND USE	DIMENSIONS
1	A, front	4″ x 13¼″
2	B and C, drawer ends	2¾″ x 11¼″
2	D and E, drawer sides	2¾″ x 10″
1	H, bottom	10″ x 12¾″
2	F and G, molding strips	½″ x 1″ x 10″

Measure, mark, square, cut, and sand each piece, as you have done for each project. If you study the working drawings carefully, you will need few directions for putting it together. You'll see that it's a simple box construction with a drawer front and molding strips added after the box has been made. Because it would be very awkward to drill from the inside of the box in order to add the front so that the screws do not show, these holes should be drilled *before* the box is assembled.

Center the end of the drawer on the front so there is ½″ at top and bottom and 1″ on each side. Draw guidelines all around the sides. Clamp the 2 pieces together. Don't nail or glue them. On the inside end of the drawer, mark the position of 3 ¾″ screws, one in the center and one toward each end.

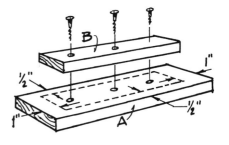

Drill through the end of the box and partway into the drawer front. Take off the clamps and redrill the holes in the end piece.

Then construct the box, using Method I.

Nail each joint with two finishing nails. Make sure the joints are square. Drill holes and put screws in each joint. Nail on the bottom.

Glue and nail a molding strip on each side, keeping the top edges of the strip even with the top edge of the drawer.

Now attach the front of the drawer. Put the screws through the holes in the end of the drawer and into the holes in the drawer front. Then from the inside, screw the end of the drawer tightly to the drawer front.

FITTING THE DRAWER IN THE CABINET OR BOOKCASE

Decide where the drawer will go before you put the cabinet or bookcase together. Then you can easily fasten the molding strips to the inside.

If the cabinet or bookcase is to be built so that the sides overlap the top, measure $2\frac{1}{4}''$ from the end of each side piece and draw a line across it. This allows $\frac{3}{4}''$ for the top of the bookcase, $\frac{1}{2}''$ for the lip of the drawer front, and $1''$ for the molding on the sides. If any of your measurements are different, be sure to add up the correct ones. If the top overlaps the sides, measure only $1\frac{1}{2}''$ from the end.

Fasten a molding strip on each side with the top edge just below the line you have

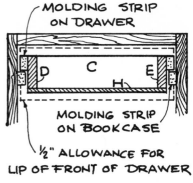

MOLDING STRIP
ON DRAWER

MOLDING STRIP
ON BOOKCASE

½" ALLOWANCE FOR
LIP OF FRONT OF DRAWER

drawn. Drill and drive 2 1″ screws about 3″ apart through the molding and into the sides. Then slide the drawer into place. Sand any edges that keep it from sliding smoothly.

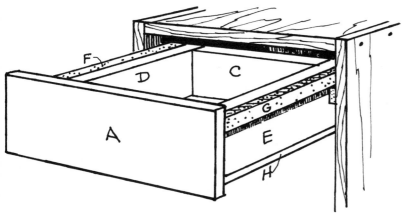

If the cabinet or bookcase has already been put together before you make the drawer, you can still fasten the molding strips inside, but doing the job at this stage will be awkward. To determine where to put the strips, measure 1½″ down from where the top meets the side.

MAKING A DESK

A piece of plywood with two bookcases or cabinets (or one of each) as bases makes a fine desk. It's a big job but not a very complicated one, since you now know how to make all of the parts involved.

First decide the size of the desk. Measure the place where you want to put it. The plans given here are for a desk 22″ x 48″ with two 15″ bases, but you can easily make it larger. However, if you decide to make it smaller, you will be able to use only one 15″ base and will have to buy legs to support the other end of the desk.

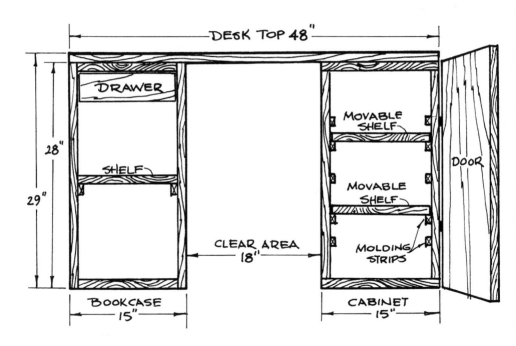

Use the bill of materials for the bookcase or cabinet (and a drawer if you want one). Add to it one piece of ¾″ plywood 22″ x 48″. Build the 2 bases and finish them (you don't need to finish the tops, which will be covered by the desk top).

Measure, mark, square, and cut the piece of plywood for the top. Finish it to match the bases. Take the 3 finished parts of the desk separately to your room or wherever the desk will be used.

Mark the location of 2 screw holes on the top of each base about 5″ from each side and halfway between front and back. Drill the holes.

Then lay the top upside down on the floor. Turn one base upside down on top of it, being sure that the outside is even with the outside edges of the top. Set the front of the base back 3″ from the front edge of the top.

If you are using a cabinet with a door, make sure the hinges are on the outside,

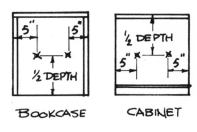

BOOKCASE   CABINET

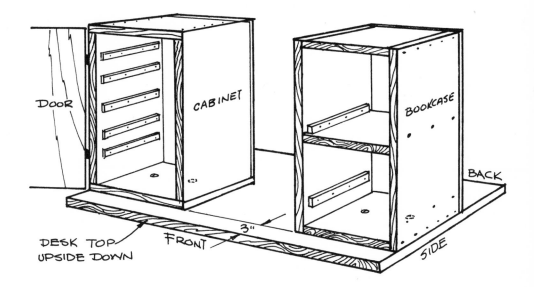

toward the end of the desk. A door that opens the wrong way is *very* inconvenient.

Have someone hold the base steady while you drill through the holes $\frac{1}{2}''$ into the plywood. If the job seems awkward, remember that even the professionals would agree with you.

Turn the base right side up and redrill the holes. Set the base upside down again. Put the screws in place and fasten them down.

Attach the other base the same way. Then have someone help you turn the desk right side up.

And both of you can admire what you've accomplished.

Part II
WOOD FINISHING

CHAPTER ONE

Choosing a Basic Finish

Putting a finish on the things you have made is the final step in working with wood and one of the most important. The finish you choose will change the appearance of even the simplest object. What you have made and the kind of wood you used will help you decide how to finish it.

Wood is composed of countless cells through which sap is carried to all parts of the tree. When the tree is sawed into lumber, these cells are exposed and many of them have been cut open. The surface cells need a finish to protect them from dirt, fingermarks, and—if the object is to be used outdoors—weather. The size and shape of these cells and the arrangement give each kind of wood its distinctive grain.

You might decide that the natural wood grain is attractive, but it would look even better in another color. You can change the color of the wood to almost any shade you want with a stain that soaks into the wood cells. Then you protect the surface with an oil finish.

If the object will receive hard use or be left outdoors, you can protect the wood with clear, colorless varnish.

However, if you have used hardboard, such as Masonite, or if the wood isn't attractive, or if it shows marks or nail holes that you couldn't hide, or just because you prefer the style, you can paint the wood in almost any color or combination of colors.

Then you can try adding a variety of creative touches to make the finish look a little different and very special.

No matter what kind of finish you plan to use, you must have the surface smooth and clean. If you sanded each piece carefully as you were putting the project together, that part of the work is nearly finished.

And if you were careful to keep your work clean, you will have no problem now. But if the wood has gotten dirty from handling, you should clean it. All the dirty marks will show through a natural finish. Paint will cover them up unless they are greasy. Try sanding to remove the marks.

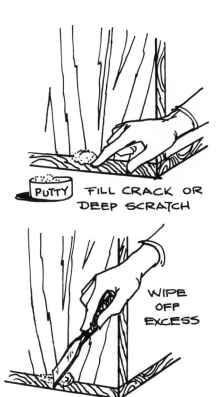

FILL CRACK OR DEEP SCRATCH

WIPE OFF EXCESS

Next, make sure all the nail holes have been filled with wood putty. If the joints don't meet perfectly, fill the cracks with wood putty. Use a putty knife to scrape off the excess. Try not to get any putty where it doesn't belong.

Unless you use a special wood putty that matches the color of the stain, the putty-filled nail holes, deep scratches, and joint cracks will show. (If there are many, you might prefer to paint the wood.)

No matter how careful you were with your tools, your hammer or screwdriver may have slipped and scratched or dented the wood. A dent means that some of the wood cells have been crushed. If you steam these crushed cells, many of them will puff up again so that most or even all of the dent will disappear.

Wet a small piece of cloth, fold it, and lay it over the dent. Then hold a hot iron over the wet cloth to make the steam. You will have to repeat this operation several times before the dent disappears.

Scratches are a different matter. A scratch is a cut, and puffing up the wood cells won't help. If the scratches are not deep, you may be able to sand them out. Remember that you must sand the area all around the scratch, too, or you will see a little hollow in the wood.

But if the scratches go deep into the wood, you will have to fill them with wood putty. Spread putty over the scratch with a knife. Start with a little more putty than you think you'll need and push it into the scratch. Then smooth out the putty and scrape off any excess from the surrounding wood. When it is dry and hard, sand it smooth.

Now make one final check for smoothness. Stretch an old nylon stocking over your hand and slide your hand over the surface. Any rough spots will snag the stocking.

There is a reason for all this careful sanding. No finish will hide rough spots. In fact, all finishes reflect light, and the more light that is reflected, the more the rough spots show. So the more time and effort you spend in getting the wood ready in the beginning, the nicer the finish will look in the end.

One thing to remember always is that *all* of the finishes and clean-up materials you will be using contain dangerous chemicals that must be handled very carefully. They

are poisonous if swallowed and can hurt your eyes if they are splashed. Some of the chemicals are irritating to the skin. Some catch fire easily. Some can make you sick if you breathe the fumes. Use them only in an airy place, and keep a window open a little even in winter.

Read all of the directions carefully and make sure you understand everything, but first you must check with an adult before you use any of these materials. Never use them or leave them around where young children are present. Always seal the cans or jars tightly, and put them away when you're finished. Be very careful about cleaning up, not only because it's unpleasant to leave a mess lying around but also because that particular mess is a fire hazard.

USING AN OIL FINISH

Sometimes, for objects that will be used around food and will be washed often, you can simply rub ordinary vegetable oil on the unfinished wood and let it soak in. Use the kind you have in the kitchen for cooking and salads or even mineral oil from the medicine chest. Use paper towels or a clean cloth to spread the oil on the wood. Add more oil as it soaks in. Let it dry for an hour or so and rub it with more paper towels to remove any excess. Put on more oil occasionally as you use and wash the object, such as the cheese board.

Vegetable and mineral oils help to protect the wood, but they don't actually seal the wood cells. For most projects, you should buy an oil-finish preparation from the paint store. Once oil finishes were made of turpentine and boiled linseed oil, a mixture that required a lot of rubbing. But now many commercial products are sold under names such as "Danish oil finish" or "antique oil finish," which are easy to use and need only a little rubbing.

On large projects, like a bookcase, work on one surface at a time. Turn the piece so that you're always working on a top surface, where the oil has a better chance to soak in.

Pour the oil from the can or bottle on a clean rag and spread the oil on the clean surface of the wood. As the oil soaks in, put more oil on the dry-looking spots. Check the directions on the container to see how long you should allow the oil to stand on the wood surface. Some oils need to be left on only 15 minutes.

Then, with a clean cloth, wipe off any oil that hasn't soaked in. If you have waited too long, the surface will be very sticky and hard to wipe. The remedy for that is simple —just put on a little more oil to dissolve the stickiness.

When the surface has dried completely, rub it well with a soft cloth to bring out the glow.

COLORING WOOD WITH STAIN

If you want to change the color of the wood and still have the pattern of the grain show through, try using a stain. Some oil stains produce natural wood colors; others are as bright as paint colors. Remember that stain only colors the wood—it doesn't protect it. After you have stained the piece, you should put a finish on it.

Oil stain comes in a can, ready to use, in a wide variety of wood colors, such as maple, walnut, and mahogany, as well as bright colors like red, blue, yellow, and green. You will need:

Stirrer: Most paint stores supply their customers with wooden paddles for stirring. You can also use a scrap of wood or even an old knife or spoon that is no longer needed in the kitchen.

Cloths: Oil stain is wiped on—and wiped off again—with clean rags or cheesecloth.

Plastic bag or rubber glove: Wear something to protect your hand from the stain, which is uncomfortably sticky when it stays on your skin.

Newspapers: Spread them under your work.

Steel wool: Very tiny steel fibers matted together in a pad are used to rub the surface before you put a protective finish on it. Use a fine grade.

Pry the lid off with a can opener, a nail, or an old knife. Don't use a screwdriver or a chisel—the tool will be ruined.

Mix the stain carefully with a stirrer, making sure that the substance that has settled to the bottom is mixed thoroughly in the liquid.

Fold a small cloth into a neat wad and dip it in the stain. Don't leave any straggly ends of cloth or threads to drag across the wood.

Always try the stain first on a scrap of the wood you used to make the object or on a hidden part of it. Then you can see how the stain will look and how long you should leave it on the wood before you start to wipe it off.

While the stain soaks into the test piece of wood, check the directions to see how long the manufacturer recommends waiting.

With a clean rag, wipe off the stain that has not soaked into the wood. Always wipe in the direction of the grain.

If you have not waited long enough before wiping, too much of the stain will come off, and the color will be very light. If you want a darker shade, you can give the wood a second coat when the first coat is dry.

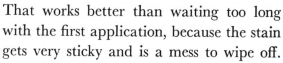

That works better than waiting too long with the first application, because the stain gets very sticky and is a mess to wipe off.

When you are satisfied with the results on the test piece, begin staining the parts of your project that are seen the least (inside, bottom) and end with the parts that are seen the most (front, top). This is customary because the parts finished last usually turn out best.

Start at one end of a section and work toward the other end.

If you are staining a small object that you can cover in the suggested waiting time, do the whole thing at once. But if you are working on a big project, stain only the parts that can be done in the recommended time. Count the waiting time from when you began staining. Then start wiping off the stain, beginning with the parts you stained first.

As soon as you have finished, soak the staining and wiping rags in water to keep them from starting a fire. Oily rags can catch fire without having a lighted match or flame anywhere near them, by spontaneous combustion. Throw the wet rags away in a closed garbage can or put them in a jar or can with a lid and throw *that* away.

When the stained surface is completely dry, rub it in the direction of the grain with fine steel wool to smooth it for the finish coat.

VARNISHING

Varnish is a very tough, clear finish. Some form of varnish has been in use for thousands of years. The ancient Egyptians decorated their tombs with it, and the Greeks varnished their ships to protect the wood from salt water. Modern furniture finishers use it on natural wood or over a coloring stain on any surface that needs good protection.

Varnish comes in a shiny finish called *gloss* and in not-so-shiny finishes like *eggshell* or *semigloss*. The duller finish is better, because it will not show every tiny speck of dust that happens to settle on it while it is drying.

There are a couple of tricks to using varnish. One is to avoid letting tiny bubbles form in it. The other is to keep your work free of dust. Bubbles and dust are the enemies of a smooth surface.

First, don't shake the can and don't stir the varnish. Either will cause bubbles, and bubbles brush right onto the surface. You hope they will disappear by themselves, but they never do. They just dry there, and the surface looks pockmarked.

Second, use a *tack rag*. Sprinkle a little varnish on a small clean cloth that is not fuzzy, such as a piece of old sheet or linen towel. Then put on rubber gloves or cover your hands with plastic bags. Squeeze and rub the rag so that the varnish works through it. Dust the wood carefully with a plain dry cloth. Then use the sticky rag to wipe the wood before you apply any coat of varnish. A tack rag picks up every last bit of dust and sawdust that could spoil the surface.

When you're not using it, be sure to keep the tack rag in a tightly closed jar, so it will not dry out and also will not start a fire.

In addition to a tack rag, you'll need:

Brush: A 1½″ nylon bristle is good.

Steel wool or sandpaper: Use a fine grade to rub the surface between coats.

Brush cleaner: Use turpentine, mineral spirits, or other chemical solvent for soaking and cleaning brushes.

VARNISH

Hold the brush as though you were holding a pencil, with the tips of your fingers on the metal band around the brush, called the *ferrule*. Dip the brush halfway into the varnish. Let some of the varnish run back into the can.

Start in the center of the section you are varnishing. Let the varnish flow off the brush and onto the surface. Work in long, even strokes from the center toward the ends. Be generous with the varnish, but not sloppy.

Then go back and forth across the surface to *cross brush* it. Don't use any more varnish—just go over the varnish you've already put on. Cross brushing helps to catch

any places you might have missed the first time, and it evens out the surface.

Let the varnish dry thoroughly. Read the directions on the can to see approximately how long it will take. Some varnishes dry faster than others. Drying takes much longer in damp weather.

If you are going to use the varnish brush again soon, stand it in a jar of turpentine, mineral spirits, or thinner to keep it from drying out and getting hard. Gently squeeze the liquid out of the brush with a rag before you use it again.

When the varnish is completely dry, rub it with fine steel wool or sandpaper. This gives the surface a "tooth" for the second coat to hold onto. Dust off the surface with a piece of old sheet or linen and go over it carefully with your tack rag to pick up all dust. Then apply a second coat.

When all your varnishing is finished, clean the brush thoroughly. Dip and stir the brush in a small amount of the cleaning liquid, and squeeze it out. Dip, stir, and squeeze again. Make sure all the varnish is out of the bristles before you dry the brush and put it away.

PAINTING

Paint is one of the most popular finishes for wood. Although it won't hide improperly sanded wood, paint will cover scratches, nail holes and joints that have been filled with wood putty, marks that won't wash off, grain, and hardboard or other surface that would look much better hidden. And you can use many different colors and color combinations.

There are two main types of paint, depending on the liquid base in which the coloring is mixed—*oil-base* paint and *water-base* paint, which is also known as *latex* paint. Water-base paint is very popular because cleaning up is so simple—you simply wash the brush with water and soap. If you get paint on your skin or clothes or splatter it around when painting, you can clean it off easily with a wet cloth. But you must clean it *before* it dries. Oil-base paints must be cleaned with turpentine or mineral spirits.

Different kinds of paints have different uses. You would not use exterior house paint, for instance, to finish a piece of furniture. *Enamel*, which has a hard, durable surface, would be fine for any of the projects in this book.

Decide whether you want a shiny finish, a dull finish, or something in between. A *gloss* paint is very shiny and is easy to keep clean. Finger marks wipe off with little effort, and the surface is not so easily marked up. But shiny finishes also show up any little flaws in the surface or any bits of dust that might float into the paint while it is drying.

Flat paint produces a dull finish. It reflects much less light than gloss, and little flaws or particles of dust don't show up. But it is not as tough as gloss.

Many people find that *semigloss* has some of the best features of gloss and flat. It has a luster, a quiet shine, that looks attractive on furniture and other objects. It is merchandised by a variety of names, such as *satin* or *eggshell* or *low luster*. A paint dealer can help you select the kind of paint that's best for your project, but, generally, just ask for *latex semigloss enamel*. There are usually dozens of colors to choose from.

You'll also need:

Brush: A 1½″ nylon bristle is good. Craftsmen who do a lot of painting buy the best available, but many people prefer inexpensive brushes so they don't have to be as careful with them.

Stirrer: If the paint store doesn't give you one, you can use an old stirrer coated with dried paint, but it must be clean. You can also use a scrap of wood or even an old knife or spoon.

Newspapers: Have a pile on hand for spreading under your work.

Masking tape: Use this to protect the areas you *don't* want to paint.

Pry open the can. With a nail, punch sev-

eral holes around the inside rim of the can so the paint that collects there can drip right back into the can.

Stir the paint thoroughly, getting all the thick substance at the bottom of the can evenly mixed.

Then study the project you are going to paint, and decide how you are going to approach it. As a general rule, you should paint first the parts you see least. Also, when you can, have the part you are painting lying down flat so that you are always painting a top surface. This position will give you a smoother finish, and there'll be less chance of runs and drips.

For example, if you are painting a bench, follow this order:

Turn it upside down and paint the underside of the top and the end pieces, or legs.

Carefully turn the bench right side up without touching the wet paint. Paint the edges and, finally, paint the top.

On some projects, you must let one painted side dry completely before you turn the piece over onto that side and proceed to the next.

Hold your paintbrush as though you were holding a pencil, with the tips of your fingers on the metal band, called the *ferrule*.

Dip half the length of the bristles into the paint. Press the soaked brush against the inside edge of the can so that some of the paint runs back into the can. You want

to keep enough paint on the brush to do the job efficiently, but not so much that it will drip and run. If you don't have enough paint, it will not go on smoothly.

Start in the center of each part and paint toward the edge. If you start at the edge and paint toward the center, the edge will collect too much paint and you'll have drips.

To make sure you haven't missed any spots, go back and forth across the surface and cross brush it.

Use the tips of the bristles to work the paint into tight corners. But don't "scrub" with the brush or press down hard on it. Just stroke lightly and smoothly with long, even strokes. If you find yourself pressing down too hard, you probably don't have enough paint on the brush.

Be sure you have plenty of good light so that you don't miss any spots.

Put on one coat of paint and let it dry thoroughly. How fast it will dry depends on the kind of paint you are using, on the temperature of the room, and on the weather. Read the directions on the can to see how long the paint usually takes to dry. Don't hurry the drying.

When the first coat is completely dry, put on the next coat. With most paints, two should be enough. But with some colors, especially very light ones, you might need to apply a third coat.

PAINTING WITH TWO COLORS

Two colors of paint can give some unusual effects that will make your work distinctly your own. For instance, you could paint a box blue on the outside and green on the inside. Or you could paint a 5-sided cube white both inside and out and the edges a bright yellow. Try to find two colors that are good contrasts.

When you apply the first color, be careful not to get it on the places where the second color will go. Use masking tape to cover the areas next to the part you are going to paint. Do all the necessary coats in the first color. When the last coat is completely dry, you're ready for the second color.

Again, use masking tape to protect the first color. Make sure the tape is stuck on firmly, so that none of the second color can leak under it and spoil the first color. When the last coat is completely dry, pull off the masking tape.

If, after all, some of the second color happens to turn up where it does not belong, paint carefully over the mistake when it is dry.

CHAPTER TWO

Adding a Decorative Finish

After you have put on a basic finish, you might like to add some unusual fancy touches. You can develop your own designs, use some of the suggestions in this chapter, or find new ideas from other sources. The important thing is to use a design and a technique that are just right for your project.

Practice some of these techniques on a piece of scrap wood until you feel sure of yourself before you tackle the finished work.

STENCILING

If you have ever tried to paint a freehand design, you know how tricky the technique can be. Even when there is an outline to follow, you need a very steady hand not to go squiggling over the edge.

One of the easier ways to paint uniform letters or designs on wood is with a stencil, which you can buy inexpensively or make yourself with thin cardboard or very stiff paper (file cards are a good weight). You will also need manicure or other small, pointed scissors, paint in a color to contrast with the basic finish, and a small stiff brush. If you will be using only small amounts of paint and have nothing on hand that seems right, you can buy little jars of acrylic paints from an art-supply store.

When you are designing a stencil, you must remember that the part to be painted is cut away. If there are inside parts of the design to be left unpainted, you must provide a way to hold those parts in place.

The letter *C,* for example, is not a problem. But if you are stenciling the letter *A, B,* or *D,* you must keep the center in place by leaving little strips of paper to connect the center to the outside of the letter.

Or you can simplify your letters by leaving out all of the centers.

Keep your designs as simple as possible and the lines smooth and even. The more tiny details you include, the harder it will be to cut the stencil neatly. Use coins, jar lids, and other objects as patterns for drawing the design, or trace outline shapes from illustrations in books or magazines.

You can stencil on the main shapes and fill in the details freehand, such as in these designs.

A round sun face is painted with a stencil, but the eyes and the smile are added separately.

Use a stencil to draw a heart, but paint *I Love You* on it by hand.

Or you can stencil on a bunch of flowers,

then add stems and extra leaves by hand.

Take time to plan your design, making sure it will fit the way you want. Cut pieces of scrap paper the same size and general shape as parts of your design and arrange them on the surface to get an idea of how they will look.

Here are two more stencil patterns you can use or that may suggest ideas of your own. Choose one that seems best for the object you are decorating. Use graph paper with ¼″ squares and copy the design, square by square, onto the graph paper. Then put a piece of carbon paper, carbon side down, between the graph paper and the stencil sheet. Trace over each line of the design with a sharp pencil.

Cut out the design with small, pointed scissors. Remember to cut out only the parts that will be painted.

Place the cut stencil exactly where you

want it on the surface and tape it in place with masking tape.

With a small, stiff brush, dab the paint on the cut-out area. To avoid getting paint under the edges, which could spoil your design, don't drag the brush across the stencil.

As you go along, press down the edges of the stencil next to the cut-out part you are painting. Leave the stencil in place while the paint dries.

GLAZING

By streaking a special **glaze** over a painted surface, you can give it a darker, richer color and a more interesting texture. A glaze is easy to use, because if you don't like the way it looks the first time, you can change it until you get the effect you want. And if you still aren't satisfied, you can simply wipe off the glaze and start over.

Glazes are sold in special kits, usually for "antiquing," which many people use to redecorate old furniture or to get unusual effects on new pieces. You can buy a kit, but you can mix your own glazes for much less money.

The color of the glaze you make depends on the color of the basic finish and on the special effect you want to create. These are the traditional tones that are used for antiquing:

Raw umber: Makes a light, brownish tone to use over white or light-colored paint, except for light blue, which it makes look greenish.

Raw sienna: Makes a warm reddish tone on light colors.

Lamp black: Makes a dull, dirty tone that should be used only on strong colors like bright red or blue or green, to deepen them.

You can also make a glaze with pure, bright colors that look very new instead of very old.

The glaze should always be darker than the basic finish. For instance, you can use dark blue or green to glaze a medium blue paint, red to glaze pink or orange, orange to glaze yellow or white, and so on.

A very sharp contrast probably would not look right. Don't glaze white paint with black or dark blue, which will make the finish look dirty. But if you mix a little white in the glaze with the black or blue, the effect will be a soft grayish tone on a white background.

You can buy a glazing liquid—a cloudy, colorless oil—at a paint store and add your color to that. Or you can mix this formula in a small glass jar. Use an old teaspoon to measure and mix the glaze:

1 spoonful artists' oil paint from a tube (use one of the colors mentioned above)

1 spoonful boiled linseed oil (you don't have
   to boil it; it comes that way)

3 spoonfuls of turpentine

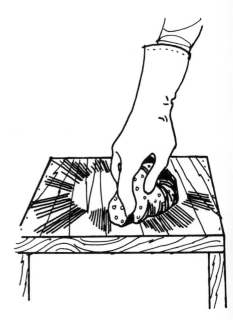

As in all painting, it's best to work on a
horizontal surface, one side at a time. The
easiest way to apply the glaze is with a rag.
Wear a rubber glove or a plastic bag to protect your hand. If you use a brush, you don't
need a glove.

Spread the glaze on generously. You don't
have to apply it in any particular way, but
try to cover the surface fairly evenly.

Begin wiping off the glaze right away.
Most people use a cloth for wiping, but you
can get unusual effects by patting the surface with a tissue. As the tissue gets soggy,
throw it away and use a fresh one.

The usual way is to wipe the center of
each section almost completely, leaving
more and more of the stain on the piece as
you get closer to the edge. Try to make the
change gradual. The glaze dries slowly, so
you will have plenty of time to do this gradual wiping, or to redo it if you want. When
it looks right, go on to the next section.

Let the glaze dry overnight. Then put on
a final coat of varnish to protect it.

DECOUPAGE

Decoupage comes from a French word
meaning "to cut out" and is the art of deco-

rating a wooden object, either painted or plain, with paper cutouts. Two hundred years ago elegant ladies in Europe spent their time decorating beautiful boxes and trays with decoupage. Some modern decoupage looks as though it were done long ago. But it is also possible to make decoupage that is very fresh, new, and original looking, and not old-fashioned at all.

Pictures for decoupage projects are cut out and pasted on the wooden surface, then "submerged"—buried under several coats of varnish until you no longer can see or feel the cut edges of the paper. The cutout picture appears to be actually painted on.

You will need:

Pictures: Use pictures cut from greeting cards, wallpaper, gift wrapping, postcards, even seed packets. The best pictures to work with are printed on fairly thin paper that has no printing on the back. Thin paper requires fewer coats of varnish to submerge. If there is printing on the back, it sometimes bleeds, or shows through the picture on the right side.

Scissors: Tiny manicure scissors are the best, but use whatever you have.

Glue: Use white household glue, like Elmer's Glue-All or Solomon's Sobo Glue.

Brayer: This small roller is useful for pressing down the glued picture, but it is not essential.

Waxed paper and paper towels: These will help you do a neat job.

Varnishing supplies: Clear varnish, brush, fine sandpaper or steel wool, and the proper brush cleaner are all necessary. You can buy special decoupage varnish or use whatever clear, colorless varnish you have on hand.

Although you can paste the decoupage pictures on unpainted or stained wood, most people like to paint the wood first. When you are deciding what color paint to use, have your decoupage picture in mind. If it is very elaborate and printed on a white background and you plan to leave on most of the background, you probably should paint the wood white. Or you might want to select one of the colors in the picture and use that color to paint the wood.

But if you have painted the object already and later decide to add a decoupage cutout, be sure to find a picture that goes with the base color.

Although decoupage means to cut out, you can also tear out the picture, especially if it is a large one with lots of tricky edges. Instead of trying to snip around each edge, simply tear all the way around.

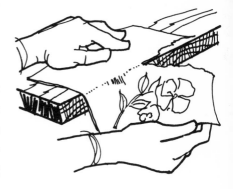

Tear the background—the part you don't want—downward. Keep turning the picture and tearing away the outer part. The edge is supposed to look uneven, so if it isn't tearing that way by itself, help it along. Tearing

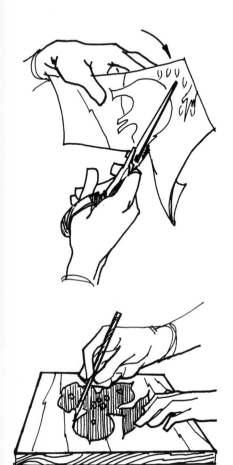

down, not up, gives the paper a better gluing edge.

Another method is to lay the picture face down on a piece of wax paper. Lay strips of wet paper towel around the edges you want to tear and let them soak for about fifteen minutes. Then pull the background gently away. The picture will have a nice feathery edge. Then let it dry.

If you decide to cut out the picture, trim away some of the outside paper that you don't want. Then start cutting as close to the design as you can. Instead of moving the scissors around the picture, hold the scissors steady and "feed" the design into the scissors. You don't have to cut around every tiny detail, but you should make the cuts smooth.

Lay the picture on the surface in the exact place you want it, and mark a few guidelines *lightly* with pencil or chalk so that you can readily see the area.

Now put the cutout face down on a piece of wax paper. Use your fingers to spread a thin coat of glue on the back of the cutout. Work quickly so that the glue doesn't dry before you are finished, but try to put the glue on evenly.

Lift the cutout from the wax paper and lay it within the guidelines. If you have a brayer, cover the picture with a damp paper towel and roll the brayer over the cutout from the center toward the edges. This pushes out the air bubbles and excess glue, which the towel will soak up.

If you don't have a brayer, pat the cutout with a slightly damp sponge or wadded paper towel. Start in the center and work toward the edges. Be sure to wipe away carefully the glue that squeezes out.

Let the glue dry at least overnight. If you varnish the decoupage when the glue is still damp, the moisture will make the varnish cloudy.

Now begin submerging the cutout under coats of clear, colorless varnish or decoupage finish. Follow the directions for varnishing on page 109. Be sure the brush is very clean, and take care not to create bubbles.

Press down gently on the brush, letting the varnish flow off onto the surface of the object. Be sure to cover the whole side on which the cutout is glued. Don't brush back and forth over the cutout; the colors might bleed or the picture become damaged.

You will probably have to put on *at least* six coats of varnish if you want the edges of the cutout to disappear so that you can't see or feel them. It is better to put on several thin coats rather than a few heavy ones. The other sides of the object need only two coats.

Each coat of varnish must dry completely before the next one is flowed on. You don't need to sand between each coat. One sanding every three coats is enough, unless there are drips or runs. The special decoupage finish probably won't need any sanding at all.

Some people like to glaze their decoupage projects. After the cutout has been submerged, follow the directions for glazing on page 121. Wipe most of the glaze off the cutout and gradually deepen the glaze toward the edges. When the glaze is dry, put two more coats of varnish over it.

Woodworking is a craft that requires careful attention to detail. Each measurement must be precise and each cut accurate. The result is a well-made object.

Preparation for finishing is painstaking work, but it is in the finishing that your most creative ideas can be expressed. After you've tried some of the suggestions in this book, experiment with your own designs and your own way of doing things. That's when you'll truly appreciate the pleasures of wood as people have for centuries.